ENGLISH
Fast Forward 2

LYNDA BERISH

SANDRA THIBAUDEAU

Collège Marie-Victorin

Prentice Hall Regents Canada, Scarborough, Ontario

Canadian Cataloguing in Publication Data

Berish, Lynda, 1952—
  English fast forward 2

ISBN 0-13-513731-4

1. English language—Textbooks for second language learners.*
I. Thibaudeau, Sandra, 1943—   . II. Title.

PE1128.B484 1995   428.2'4   C95-931966-2

Prentice-Hall, Inc., Englewood Cliffs, New Jersey
Prentice-Hall International, Inc., London
Prentice-Hall of Australia, Pty., Ltd., Sydney
Prentice-Hall of India Pvt., Ltd., New Delhi
Prentice-Hall of Japan, Inc., Tokyo
Prentice-Hall of Southeast Asia (Pte.) Ltd., Singapore
Editora Prentice-Hall do Brasil Ltda., Rio de Janeiro
Prentice-Hall Hispanoamericana, S.A., Mexico

ISBN 0-13-513731-4

Executive editor: Clifford J. Newman
Managing editor: Marta Tomins
Production editor: Elynor Kagan
Production coordinator: Anita Boyle
Design and layout: Joseph Chin
Illustrations: David Shaw
Cover design: Alex Li

Printed and bound in Canada

 2 3 4 5   99 98 97

Contents

TO THE TEACHER   v

ACKNOWLEDGEMENTS   vii

TOPIC	GRAMMAR	LISTENING ACTIVITIES
Getting Started 1	Present Simple and Present Continuous	1. Nice To Run Into You
UNIT 1 **Communication** 15	Present Tense Questions	2. Meeting Friends
UNIT 2 **The Food We Eat** 27	Requesting Permission	3. Let's Order In
UNIT 3 **Your Finances** 37	WH-Question Words	4. Opening a Bank Account 5. Never Trust a Stranger Episode 1: Making Plans
UNIT 4 **The Weather** **Wherever You Go** 51	Simple Past Tense	6. Clearing the Snow in Montreal 7. Never Trust a Stranger Episode 2: Dorval Airport
UNIT 5 **What's Happening to** **Our Environment?** 67	Past Continuous Tense Adverbs with *How* and *Why*	8. The Sloth 9. Never Trust a Stranger Episode 3: Meeting Julie
UNIT 6 **Sports In Our Lives** 81	Gerunds	10. Joining the Y 11. Never Trust a Stranger Episode 4: Paul Hawke
UNIT 7 **Fads and Fashions** 93	Present Perfect Aspect (1): Duration of Time	12. The Mystery of Bruce Lee 13. Never Trust a Stranger Episode 5: A Surprise Call

UNIT 8
Technology 105
	Present Perfect Aspect (2):
	Indefinite Past Time
		14. Chester Carlson's Marvellous
		   Machine
		15. Never Trust a Stranger
		   Episode 6: Ticket to the Temple

UNIT 9 **Emergency** 119	*Will* for Future Time	16: Calling 911 17: Never Trust a Stranger Episode 7: Too Many Coincidences

UNIT 10
Getting Married   **131**

Be going to for Future Time

18. Niagara Falls
19. Never Trust a Stranger
    Episode 8: The Police Station

UNIT 11
Health and Medicine   **145**

Giving Advice Using *Should*
Expressing Obligation Using
Have to

20. Medical Emergencies
21. Never Trust a Stranger
    Episode 9: Epiloque

UNIT 12
The Great Outdoors   **159**

Conditional Sentences (Type 1)

22. Moose on the Loose

APPENDIX 1   **173**

Spelling Verb Forms Ending "ing"

APPENDIX 2   **174**

Spelling Simple Past Tense

APPENDIX 3   **175**

Irregular Past Tense and Past Participle Forms

To the Teacher

The *English Fast Forward* Series

The *English Fast Forward* series is designed for young adults learning English for work, career, or college-education purposes. It is a dynamic blend of imaginative interactive activities. Whole-language and grammar activities are treated thematically with the interests of college-age students in mind.

Fast Forward 2 is aimed at students who have studied basic English but continue to have difficulty communicating in the language. Activities in the text are designed to encourage students to develop their listening comprehension and to express themselves in spoken and written English.

The Activities

Each of the 12 units in the book consists of challenging and interesting reading passages together with stimulating and varied interaction activities. Listening activities include dialogues and listening passages. A dynamic feature of *Fast Forward 2* is a 9-part mini-series, "Never Trust a Stranger," that gives students extensive listening practice and the opportunity to develop vocabulary, discussion, and writing skills. Suggestions for speaking and writing assignments are based on themes in the book. The "Grammar Close-Up" sections provide innovative grammar practice in each unit. The addition of quizzes, puzzles, and games makes a complete package from which to choose activities for each lesson.

Teacher's Manual

A complete teacher's manual accompanies each book in the series. The manual for *English Fast Forward 2* contains several features that will be appreciated by any classroom teacher. Photocopyable masters are provided for a first-day introductory unit. Step-by-step instructions are keyed to the student book. A wealth of suggestions is provided for getting the most out of each of the units. A complete answer key for all activities as well as tape scripts for all listening passages are included in the teacher's manual.

Detailed teacher's notes are also provided to make the intention of the activities clear and to guide new teachers. Experienced teachers will find that the material is complete and flexible and can be readily adapted to accommodate individual teaching styles.

Achievement Tests

Photocopyable achievement tests are provided in the teacher's manual to evaluate student's progress. They follow the format and themes of the book and test for listening, reading, and writing. Suggestions are made for ways to test oral production on an on-going basis using marking grids from the test package.

The authors wish success and satisfaction to their colleagues and to the students who use these materials.

Lynda Berish
Sandra Thibaudeau

Acknowledgements

We would like to express our appreciation to administrators and colleagues at CEGEP Marie-Victorin for their support and collaboration. Thanks go to Mme. Nicole Simard, André Charbonneau, and Sandra Koop.

Several people offered particular encouragement for the *Fast Forward* project: Yolanda de Rooy, Cliff Newman, Marta Tomins, Kedre Murray, and Kelly Shaw. Our thanks go to them. Thank you also to Daniel Feist and Joe Chin for their technical expertise and to Elynor Kagan for her invaluable editorial assistance.

Special thanks go to Margaret Chell for her continuing support, and to Chuck Pearo and Daniel Boulerice for their lively contribution to the listening program.

Many thanks also to our husbands and children for their patience and good humour, to Millicent and Max Goldman for their encouragement and proofreading skills, and to Pie-Yuan Han and Vernetta Oberoi for keeping us on our feet.

Getting Started

Let Me Introduce...
Interaction

Greeting Customs
Reading

Nice To Run Into You
Listening Activity 1

Close-Up on Idioms
How Do You Say It?

Grammar Close-Up
Present Simple Tense

Grammar Close-Up
Present Continuous Tense

Going Abroad
What's the Difference?
Vocabulary

Let Me Introduce...

Work with a partner. Read the questions and answer according to what you usually do.

1. When you meet someone new, the first thing you say is:
   a) "What is your name?"
   b) "It's nice to meet you."
   c) "Who are you?"

2. When you and an old friend meet on the street, you probably:
   a) shake hands with each other
   b) hug and kiss each other
   c) slap each other on the back

3. When you arrive for a job interview, you:
   a) give your name in a loud, clear voice
   b) ask the interviewer to give his or her name
   c) give your name and say why you are there

4. The statement "I'd like you to meet my friend..." means that you want to:
   a) greet a friend
   b) introduce someone
   c) ask to meet someone

5. You usually shake hands:
   a) when you arrive at a party
   b) when you arrive for class
   c) when you meet someone new

6. When you meet a teacher outside school, you:
   a) say, "Hi, teacher."
   b) smile and say, "Hello."
   c) look in the other direction

7. When you are with two people who don't know each other, you:
   a) take turns asking them questions
   b) introduce them to each other
   c) talk about yourself to break the ice

8. You would kiss someone on both cheeks in greeting if he or she were:
   a) your boyfriend or girlfriend
   b) a close relative of yours
   c) a classmate from school

Greeting Customs

A. Read the text and answer the questions.

The custom of shaking hands probably began in the distant past when people lived in small clans or villages. People in those times were often suspicious of strangers because outsiders were sometimes armed and dangerous. A good way for two people to show that they weren't armed was to show their open hands when they met. That sign reassured both of them, and they took each other's hands to signal friendship. The custom of handshaking still exists as a form of greeting today.

Shaking hands is considered a polite gesture in many circumstances nowadays. People generally extend their hands when they are introduced. In business contexts, people generally shake hands to conclude discussions or to seal agreements. Politicians shake hands to give the impression of openness, warmth, and honesty. Officials usually shake hands when they give out awards or congratulations.

There are several variations in handshaking styles. Some people just touch hands lightly and let go. Other people have a firm grip and shake hands vigorously. Old friends may shake their hands a few more times than casual friends or acquaintances. A close friend may use two hands to take someone's hand as a special sign of friendship.

In social situations, handshaking is common. Friends shake hands when they meet or when they wish to say goodbye to each other. The host or hostess at a party exchanges handshakes with guests as they arrive or depart. Among close friends or on special occasions, handshaking may be accompanied by an embrace or by kissing both cheeks.

Among the Inuit in northern Canada, the traditional greeting was not handshaking, but touching noses. Some people think that the reason for this tradition was the climate. In very cold weather, it may have been easier to rub noses than to remove gloves and shake hands.

Questions

1. Why were people in the ancient clans suspicious of outsiders?
2. How did strangers reassure each other when they met?
3. What did taking someone's hand signal?
4. Name three situations where handshaking is customary today.
5. Describe two variations in how people shake hands.
6. What are two variations in handshaking customs between old friends?
7. Name two circumstances in which people shake hands socially.
8. What gestures may accompany handshaking in social situations?
9. What greeting custom is associated with the Inuit?
10. What explanation is offered for the custom?

B. Find these words in the story. Then match the words that have a similar meaning.

1. a meeting		a)	a gesture
2. friends		b)	to hold
3. firm		c)	acquaintances
4. a sign		d)	generally
5. circumstances		e)	strong
6. to embrace		f)	a tradition
7. to grip		g)	situations
8. a custom		h)	strangers
9. outsiders		i)	to hug
10. usually		j)	an encounter

Nice To Run Into You

Listening Activity 1

A. Read the short text below. Then close your book and listen as your teacher dictates. While you listen, try to write exactly what you hear.

Small talk is chatting for social reasons. Two or more people who find themselves together usually make small talk. Someone makes a comment about a common, everyday subject, and then other people follow up by asking questions or giving their opinions on the topic. Then someone else takes a turn by introducing another similar topic and the conversation continues.

B. First, read the questions aloud with a partner. Then listen to the conversation and answer the questions.

1. Where did Daniel and Diane meet?

   _____

2. How did Daniel and Paul meet?

   _____

3. What is Paul studying at the college?

   _____

4. Why is Diane happy to learn that Paul has a part-time job at the Bay?

   _____

5. What does Paul suggest that Diane do?

   _____

6. What is Diane studying at the college?

   _____

7. What does Daniel like about his math teacher?

   _____

8. What does he not like about his math teacher?

   _____

9. Why did Daniel not go out for basketball this year?

   _____

Turn to page 12 for Exercise C.

Close-Up on Idioms: How Do You Say It?

Use these idioms to replace the expressions in bold in the sentences. Write out the sentences using the new expressions.

a) Long time, no see.
b) some time to kill
c) No kidding!
d) an opening

e) is too heavy on the…
f) blow it
g) ran into/bumped into

1. I have **a little extra time** before my next class. Do you want to go out for lunch?
2. I think the book store has a **job available**. Why don't you apply?
3. Hi, everyone. How are you? **I haven't seen you in a long time**.
4. Bob and Martin are in the same class? **I'm surprised!** I didn't know that.
5. My friend Annie cooks very well, but sometimes her food **has a little too much** salt.
6. Guess who I **met** yesterday? My old friend Lise.
7. My exam was really hard. I hope I didn't **fail it**.

Grammar Close-Up: Present Simple Tense

Use the present simple tense to describe habitual actions or things in nature that don't change.

> EXAMPLES: I take a bus to school every day.
>
> The sun rises in the east.

Affirmative
I take
you take
he takes
she takes
it takes
we take
you take
they take

The present simple tense uses the base form of the verb. The exception is the third person singular (**he, she, it**) form that adds **s** or **es** to the base form of the verb.

EXAMPLES: He likes English. She goes to college.

Negative

Add **do not** before the base form of the main verb to make the negative form.

> EXAMPLES: I know.
>
>   I **do not** know.

When the subject is **he**, **she** or **it**, use **does not** before the base form of the main verb. For the negative form of the third person singular, *do not* add **s** or **es** to the main verb.

> EXAMPLE: ✔ He does not know.
>
>   ✗ He does not knows.

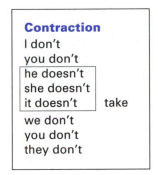

Negative		**Contraction**	
I do not		I don't	
you do not		you don't	
he does not		he doesn't	
she does not		she doesn't	
it does not	take	it doesn't	take
we do not		we don't	
you do not		you don't	
they do not		they don't	

A. Change the statements to the negative form. Use contractions.

1. In the winter I drive to school.
2. It takes a long time to get downtown.
3. The subway opens at six o'clock.
4. Mei and Karen leave for class at the same time.
5. Vancouver and Kyoto have subway systems.
6. Bob goes to work by public transportation.
7. Miguel likes to walk to school.
8. Suzanne and Tania live in the same building.
9. The bus leaves at exactly 8:15.
10. Mike rides his bike to class in the winter.

B. Look at the affirmative and negative sentences with the present simple tense. Find the errors and correct them.

1. Jean walk to school every day.
2. Anne don't drive to school.
3. They takes the bus sometimes.
4. Bob Martin have a new car.
5. The bus sometimes come late.
6. We don't likes the subway.
7. Fred drive to work.
8. You don't likes to take the bus.
9. She doesn't needs a car.
10. They rides their bicycles to class.

Grammar Close-Up: Present Continuous Tense

The continuous aspect describes how an action takes place. It focuses on the moment that something is happening.

Use the present continuous for actions that are in progress now.

> EXAMPLE: I am standing at the bus stop.

Use the present continuous for temporary situations.

> EXAMPLE: They are travelling in South America at the moment.

To form the present continuous, put the auxiliary verb **be** before the main verb. Add **ing** to the main verb. Note that the ending **ing** shows continuous action. The auxiliary verb (**am**, **is**, or **are**) shows present time.

Note: For rules on spelling the present continuous, see the chart in Appendix 1, page 173.

Affirmative		**Contraction**	
I am		I'm	
you are		you're	
he is		he's	
she is		she's	
it is	standing	it's	standing
we are		we're	
you are		you're	
they are		they're	

Choose the correct verbs to complete the description of the picture. Put the verbs in the present continuous form.

wait   cook   read   stand   have   sit   pour   make   hold   put

This is a picture of Mother's Day at my house. My mother

1_____ at the table. She **2**_____ the news-

paper. My father is at the stove. He **3**_____ some eggs.

My younger sister **4**_____ flowers on the table. They are

a surprise for mother. My older brother **5**_____ at the

counter. He **6**_____ coffee into two mugs. I am at the

counter too. I **7**_____ toast. I **8**_____ for the

toast to be ready. My older sister **9**_____ a package. It is

a Mother's Day present. We **10**_____ a good time.

 In English, the verb **have** is used in expressions such as **have a bath**, **have a good time**, **have a coffee**, **have a baby**, **have an exam**.

Present Continuous Negative

Put **not** after the auxiliary verb **be**. Use the **ing** form of the main verb to show continuous action. The auxiliary verb (**am**, **is**, or **are**) shows that the action is in present time. Use the auxiliary verb **be** + **not** to form negation with the continuous aspect.

EXAMPLE: They **are not going** to the party.

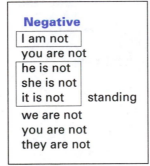
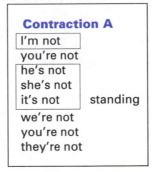

Negative
I am not
you are not
he is not
she is not
it is not   standing
we are not
you are not
they are not

Contraction A
I'm not
you're not
he's not
she's not
it's not   standing
we're not
you're not
they're not

Contraction B
✗
you aren't
he isn't
she isn't
it isn't   standing
we aren't
you aren't
they aren't

Write these sentences in the negative form. Use contractions.

1. Maria is taking math this semester.
2. Bob is meeting us at the theatre.
3. The team is playing out of town this week.
4. The students are studying for an exam.
5. We are having a picnic on Friday.
6. Franco is waiting on the corner.
7. My sisters are trying to learn judo.
8. The teacher is speaking clearly.
9. They are running for the bus.
10. I am chewing gum.

Present Simple and Present Continuous in Contrast

Use the present simple tense to describe habitual actions.

EXAMPLE: He goes to work every day.

Another use is to describe things in nature or life that don't change.

EXAMPLE: Tigers eat meat.

Use the continuous aspect to describe actions that take place as we speak.

EXAMPLE: He is sitting over there.

Another use is to describe actions that we know about at the time they happen.

EXAMPLE: They are having a math exam today.

A. Choose the present simple or the present continuous.

1. a) He is running for the train every day.
   b) He runs for the train every day.

2. a) She likes to take the subway to work.
   b) She is liking to take the subway to work.

3. a) The students are walking to class every day.
   b) The students walk to class every day.

4. a) They go to the swimming pool in the summer.
   b) They are going to the swimming pool in the summer.

5. a) My sister is working at the bank downtown this week.
   b) My sister works at the bank downtown this week.

6. a) The children get ready for school now.
   b) The children are getting ready for school now.

7. a) Please open the door, the doorbell is ringing.
   b) Please open the door, the doorbell rings.

8. a) People are usually standing in line at the bus stop.
   b) People usually stand in line at the bus stop.

9. a) They are not home now because they are travelling in Europe.
   b) They are not home now because they travel in Europe.

10. a) I'm liking my new job with the bus company.
    b) I like my new job with the bus company.

B. Complete the paragraphs with the correct form of the verbs.

Susan __1_____ (work) downtown. Usually she
__2_____ (drive) her car to work. This morning she is in
the subway. She __3_____ (look) at her watch. She
__4_____ (like) to arrive for work on time.

Tony usually _____**5**_____ (walk) to work. Today he _____**6**_____ (take) the bus. A lot of people _____**7**_____ (stand) at the bus stop. It _____**8**_____ (rain). People _____**9**_____ (hold) up their umbrellas. Tony _____**10**_____ (want) to go home and sleep.

C. These sentences are in the present simple or the present continuous. Write the sentences in the negative. Be careful to choose the correct form.

1. The bus company has 50 buses on the road.
2. The buses serve all the people in the city.
3. Tony drives a bus on the weekends.
4. Tony is working for the bus company at the moment.
5. He wants to drive a bus all his life.
6. Susanna is learning Tony's route.
7. She wants to work during the week.
8. They like to work at night.
9. The bus company asks her to work on Sundays.
10. Susanna is thinking about getting a new job.

Going Abroad: What's the Difference?

Choose the best words to complete the text.

Most people can tell you the **1**_____ between good

(same, difference, time)

manners and bad manners. It's good manners to say "Please" and

"Thank you." It's bad manners to **2**_____ when you get onto

(push, drive, wait)

the bus or to blow cigarette smoke in someone's **3**_____ .

(car, face, house)

Some customs, such as **4**_____ friends, are not so

(seeing, greeting, smiling)

universal. In Mexico, Rome, or Montreal, friends often greet each

other with a **5**_____ embrace. In Tokyo, Düsseldorf, or

(warm, funny, new)

Vancouver, a public embrace is rare. Friends shake hands, bow, or

simply smile. It is very **6**_____ that they will hug and

(strange, sure, unlikely)

kiss in public.

A team of sociologists who studied **7**_____ in

(couples, times, books)

restaurants around the world, discovered that they too had

different **8**_____ . Scientists looked at how often dinner

(ideas, jobs, habits)

partners touched each other in the space of one hour. In London,

9_____ made zero contacts per hour. In Toronto,

(actors, people, operators)

there were two contacts per hour. In Paris, dinner partners

10_____ each other 110 times per hour, and in Caracas, the

(told, saw, touched)

total rose to 180 touches per hour. What a varied world we live in!

Nice To Run Into You

C. Listen to the conversation and write the missing words.

Daniel: Hi, Paul. Nice to see you. _____ it going?

Paul: Great Daniel. How about you? Long time, no see.

Daniel: Hey, _____ you know Diane? We're in the
same math class. Diane, _____ is my friend
Paul. We played basketball on same team last year.

Paul: Nice to meet you, Diane.

Diane: Pleased to meet you too, Paul. Are you _____
student at the college this year?

Paul: Yes, I'm in humanities. But right now _____
killing some time before I start work. I _____
a part-time job at the Bay.

Diane: You work at the Bay? No kidding. _____
looking for a job on Saturdays. Do you think they
_____ any openings?

Paul: Sure. Why _____ you apply? What are you
studying, by the way?

Diane: I'm in physics. _____ why I'm in Daniel's
math class.

Daniel: Yeah. What _____ course! Math is really
tough this year. The only good thing is we _____
a great teacher. He really knows how _____
explain things well. He's a little heavy on the homework,
but I really like _____.

Diane: You guys seem _____ know each other from
basketball. Did you play on _____ college
team together last year?

Paul: Yeah. Daniel is a really good player. We're sorry
_____ isn't on the team this year.

Daniel: I miss it, but I've _____ a heavy program.
I don't want to blow it in math and _____ to
take it over again.

Paul: Yeah, I know what you mean. Well anyway, nice to run
_____ you again. Nice to meet you, Diane.
Good luck at _____ Bay. I hope you get a job.

Diane: Thanks, Paul.

Daniel: Yeah, good to see you, Paul. I hope we bump into
_____ other soon.

D. Work in groups of three. Practise reading the dialogue.

Communication

1

Keeping in Touch
Discussion

On the Phone
Discussion

Snapshots
Reading: Scanning

Pronunciation Close-Up
Word Stress

Grammar Close-Up
Question Form
   Present Simple Tense
   Present Continuous Tense

Meeting Friends
Listening Activity 2

Small Talk
Discussion

About Me
Writing

Going Abroad
Across Time and Distance
Vocabulary

Keeping in Touch

How do you communicate with the people in your life? Check (✔)
the ways that apply to you.

	Write letters	Communicate by modem	Talk on the phone	Send a fax	Get together	Send a note	Send pictures	Send gifts
your best friend								
your siblings								
good friends								
acquaintances								
your parents								
your grandparents								
your cousins								
your classmates								
your teammates								
registrars in schools								
employers								
co-workers								

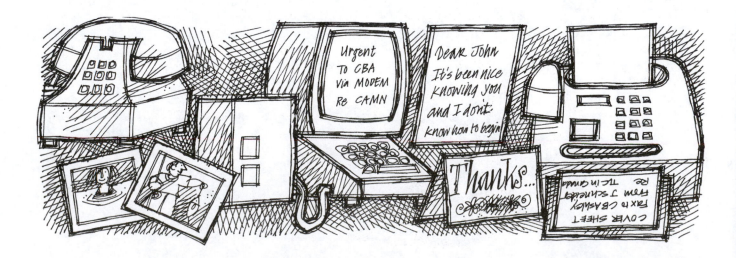

On the Phone

Did you know that the average person in North America spends two years of his or her life on the telephone?

A. Discuss these questions.

1. How much time to you spend on the phone every day?
2. How many calls do you generally make in a day?
3. Who do you speak to on the phone most often?
4. What is the length of the average call you make?
5. What was the longest phone call you ever made?
6. How often do you call long distance? Who do you call?
7. What was the most expensive long-distance phone call you ever made?

B. Do you have any special telephone services? Read about some services that are available, and discuss why people would want them.

Call Waiting

This is also called a double line. When you are talking on the phone, you may hear a beep on the line. You can press the hang-up button and answer the second call while the first caller waits on the line.

Call Forwarding

If you are away from home, you can program your phone to ring in another house or apartment temporarily. Then, when you return, you can program the phone to ring at home again.

Call Display

Telephones with this feature show which number each call is coming from. Some phones also display the name of the caller.

Conference Call

This service lets you speak to more than one person at a time. To make a conference call, you put the first person on hold and call a second person. Then you reconnect with the first person, and have a three-way conversation.

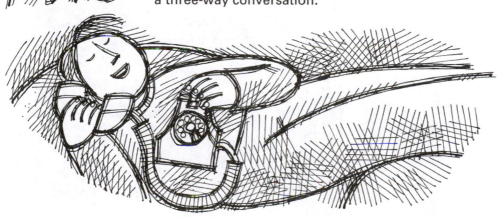

Snapshots

A. Discuss these questions.

1. Do you carry any pictures with you in your wallet or purse?
2. Who is in the pictures?
3. What kind of pictures do people put in a photo album?
4. Do you take snapshots when you go on holiday? What do you like to photograph?
5. When was the last time you took a picture? What did you photograph?
6. Did you ever have problems with a picture that you tried to take?
7. Describe the best picture you ever took.

B. Work with a partner. Find these parts of the camera.

lens
viewfinder
film-advance wheel
counter
shutter-release button
film

C. Here are the instructions from the back of a Kodak FunSaver Panoramic 35 mm camera.

Work with a partner. Read the information. Then find the answers to the questions that follow.

Reprinted Courtesy of Eastman Kodak Company.

Operating Your Camera

- Use outdoors on sunny to partly cloudy days.
- Stand with the sun behind you for best results.
- Stand at least 3 feet from your subject.

- When you are ready to take a picture, wind the FILM ADVANCE wheel in the direction of the arrow until it stops. The COUNTER indicates the number of EXPOSURES remaining.
- When you have taken the last picture, wind the FILM ADVANCE wheel until the COUNTER reads "0".

- Locate your subject in the VIEWFINDER. Actual print image (black box) is larger than scene framed in VIEWFINDER (red box).
- To correctly aim the camera, centre small circle inside large circle.
- Hold the camera steady and press the SHUTTER RELEASE button gently.

How to Develop

- Return this camera to a photo dealer for processing.
- Do not open the camera carton at any time.
- This camera will not be returned to you after photo finishing.

What You Should Know

- As part of our environmental action program, film processors are asked to return this camera to Kodak for recycling.
- Avoid exposure to water, sand, dust, and protect from heat.
- Colour dyes may change over time. Therefore, develop your film promptly.

1. How far should the photographer be from the subject?
2. The size of your picture will be smaller than what you see from the viewfinder. True (**T**) or False (**F**)?
3. To aim the camera correctly, the small circle should be inside the large circle. **T F**
4. What does the counter number tell you?
5. Why are film processors asked to return the cameras to Kodak?
6. What weather conditions are best for taking pictures?
7. Why should the film be developed right away?
8. You can develop the film yourself. **T F**
9. The sun should be behind the subject for best results. **T F**
10. What do you press to take the picture?
11. What can damage the film or the camera?
12. After the film is developed, the camera will be returned to you. **T F**

Pronunciation Close-Up: Word Stress

Choose the syllable that has the primary stress in the words below.

EXAMPLE: phótograph

1. telephone
2. employer
3. distance
4. apartment
5. direction
6. damage
7. different
8. communicate
9. paragraph
10. bicycle
11. program
12. Wednesday

Grammar Close-Up: Question Form

Present Simple Tense

To ask a question in the present simple tense, use **do** or **does** before the subject. Put a question mark (**?**) at the end of the sentence.

EXAMPLES: Do you take the bus to work?
　　　　　　Does she walk to work?

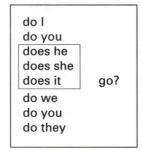

do I
do you
does he
does she
does it　　go?
do we
do you
do they

A. Read the paragraph Karen wrote. Answer the questions with forms such as, "Yes, she does," "No, they don't," etc. Correct the information where necessary.

EXAMPLE:
Do people in the city all go to work in the same way?
No, they don't. They go to work in different ways.

There are many big cities in the world. People in the city go to work in different ways. When the sun rises in the east, people in big cities usually wake up early and get ready for the day. People go to their jobs or classes by different means of transportation. My neighbour works downtown. He goes to work by car. I don't like to drive at rush hour so I usually walk a few blocks to the bus stop. Then I take the bus to work. A student lives in the apartment next door. She rides her bicycle in spring, summer, and fall. She goes to class by subway in winter.

Questions

1. Does the sun rise in the west?
2. Do people in big cities usually wake up early?
3. Do all the people who work downtown go by bus?
4. Does the neighbour walk to work?
5. Does Karen ride a bicycle to the bus stop?
6. Does Karen drive a car to work?
7. Does Karen get the bus in front of her house?
8. Does the student live in a house?
9. Does the student usually ride her bicycle to class?
10. Does the student ride her bicycle in the winter?

B. Write a question for each sentence. Use the question words to help you.

1. Annie works in a cafe as a cook.

   Where _____.

2. She works on Fridays and Saturdays.

   When _____.

3. She likes her job because it is interesting.

   Why _____.

4. She works behind the counter.

   Where _____.

5. She makes sandwiches for the customers.

   What _____.

6. When the sandwiches are ready she calls the server.

   Who _____.

7. The server carries the sandwiches to the table.

   Where _____.

8. Many customers order coffee.

   What _____.

9. Annie makes the coffee in the kitchen.

   Where _____.

10. Annie and the server leave late on Saturdays.

    When _____.

Present Continuous Tense

Put the auxiliary verb **be** before the subject to form questions. Use the **ing** form of the main verb. Put a question mark (**?**) at the end of the sentence.

EXAMPLES: You are waiting for me.
           Are you waiting for me?

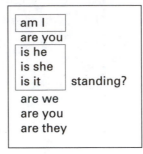

am I
are you
is he
is she
is it   standing?
are we
are you
are they

Change the statements to questions.

1. Annie is studying fashion design.
2. Robert is taking two math courses this term.
3. We are having an English exam on Wednesday.
4. Many students are missing from class this week.
5. Students are choosing their courses this week.
6. Nicole is writing the homework in her notebook.
7. I am taking too many courses this semester.
8. They are giving a presentation in the next class.
9. She is studying in the library.
10. We are being evaluated by the teacher on Friday.

 Meeting Friends

Listening Activity 2

A. Read the questions aloud with a partner. Then listen and answer the questions.

1. Where was Annie before she bumped into Marc?

   _____

2. What is she doing now?

   _____

3. Why do she and Pat like to take the bus together?

   _____

4. What program is Marc in?

   _____

5. Why does Annie think he will do well?

_____

6. What part of the program does Marc think will be hard?

_____

7. What program is Annie in?

_____

8. What does Annie think she wants to specialize in?

_____

9. What is she worried about if she stays in this program?

_____

10. What does her mother think?

_____

11. Why didn't she agree with her suggestion?

_____

12. What was Marc nervous about before he heard from the college?

_____

13. Why does Marc have to leave?

_____

B. Circle the expression that matches.

1. How's it going?
   a) What's happening?
   b) Where are you going?

2. We're supposed to...
   a) We want to...
   b) We plan to...

3. twice
   a) two times
   b) over there

4. I can't wait.
   a) I'm in a hurry.
   b) I can't understand.

5. be good at
   a) have talent
   b) try hard

6. I'm kind of...
   a) I like that kind...
   b) I'm a little bit...

7. to go into something
   a) to walk into a place
   b) to study for something

8. to live up to expectations
   a) to be what you hope it will be
   b) to live in a high place

9. I have to run.
   a) I'm in a hurry.
   b) I have to exercise.

10. Nice to see you.
    a) Nice to meet you.
    b) Nice to look at you.

Turn to page 25 for Exercise C.

Small Talk

A. Work in pairs. Look at the list of conversation topics. Put an ✗ beside the ones that are not good subjects to bring up with people you don't know well.

health	school classes
the weather	current events
sports	cars
jobs or work	clothes
family	politics
religion	money
food	teachers
people you both know	salaries
people's ages	

B. Choose three topics you find interesting. Work with a partner and write three good questions you could ask in a conversation about each of your choices.

C. Find a new partner and practise small talk on your topics. Use your questions to help you.

About Me

Write about yourself. Use these questions to help you.

1. Why did you decide to go to college?
2. What courses are you taking?
3. Which courses do you like best so far?
4. Is college different from high school? In what ways?
5. Have you had any problems adjusting to college? What are they?
6. What do you plan to do after college?

Going Abroad: Across Time and Distance

Use the words below to complete the paragraphs on page 25.

**ancestors   books   fax   paper   drawings   thoughts
offices   satellite   telegrams   distances**

One of the earliest ways human beings had of communicating through messages was cave painting. Our early ancestors left __1_____ on the walls of caves to tell about successful hunts. Later, the ancient Egyptians used pictograms to pass on legends about gods. The Chinese were the first people to use __2_____ and ink. They used complex characters to write. In Europe, the invention of the printing press made it possible to mass produce __3_____ and to preserve people's __4_____ for future generations to read.

Today, technology is compressing time and shrinking __5_____. We used to marvel at telegrams and air mail. Now things are changing so quickly that we consider news reels and __6_____ to be older technologies. We have new technologies like modems and __7_____ machines

This is an age when messages can be sent between __8_____ or even continents in seconds. News reports can be broadcast live across the globe by __9_____. Human beings are living with methods of communication that our __10_____ never dreamed of.

Meeting Friends

C. Listen to the conversation and write the missing words.

Marc: Hey Annie. How's it going?

Annie: Oh hi, Marc. _____ OK. I just got through with registration and I'm waiting for Pat. We're supposed _____ take the bus together.

Marc: Do you live near _____ other?

Annie: Yeah, we live in the same area. It's _____ long ride home. We have to change buses twice so _____ nice to have company. How are you?

Marc: Not bad. I got the courses I wanted.

Annie: What program _____ you in anyway?

Marc: I'm taking architectural design. I _____ wait to start classes. I hear it _____ amazing teachers.

Annie: You'll be good at design. You could always draw really well.

Marc: Well, there's more to it _____ drawing you know. The technical stuff is really hard. But you're right; being able to draw will _____.

Annie: I'm in social science. You should _____ seen the line-up at registration. I hope my classes _____ too big.

Marc: Yeah, a lot of people are going into social science. What are you going to specialize _____?

Annie: I'm not _____. I'm kind of leaning toward anthropology, but there might not be much work available. My mom _____ me to go into nursing, but I'm pretty weak in math. Anyway, I _____ always switch next session if I change my mind.

Marc: I'm sure about my program. _____ wanted to do it since I was a kid, but I wasn't sure _____ get in. I can't tell you how happy I was to get _____ letter of acceptance from the college.

Annie: It sounds good. I hope it lives _____ to your expectations.

Marc: Me too. Anyway, I guess I can also change later if I need _____. Well Annie, I have to run. I've got a part-time job and my shift starts in half an hour.

Annie: Where _____ you working?

Marc: At the drug store. It's not as bad _____ it sounds. Say hi to Pat.

Annie: Sure Marc. _____ to see you again. 'Bye.

Marc: See ya.

D. Practise the dialogue with a partner.

E. Write a new dialogue about meeting a friend. Use the vocabulary and expressions from this unit to help you.

The Food We Eat

2

Fast Food
Discussion
Vocabulary

Let's Order In
Listening Activity 3

Ordering Supper
Role Play

Granola
Reading

Grammar Close-Up
Requesting Permission

Going Abroad
Pizza Pie
Vocabulary

Fast Food

A. Discuss these questions about fast food.

1. What kind of snacks do you like to eat?
2. What does the term "fast food" refer to? Give examples.
3. Is fast food the same thing as junk food?
4. What kind of food is healthy?
5. Can fast food be healthy?

B. Look at the pictures. Find things that you eat or drink in the following ways:

1. in a bun
2. with ketchup
3. hot
4. cold
5. with a straw
6. with onions
7. with your fingers
8. at the movies
9. as a meal
10. as a snack
11. from a bag
12. with a fork
13. with sauce
14. as a dessert
15. with a spoon
16. with salt
17. with mustard
18. with cheese

Let's Order In

Listening Activity 3

A. Read the paragraph. Then close your book and write as the teacher dictates.

We like to order in for different reasons. Some people order in because they are too tired to cook dinner after a long day. Some people order in when they are in a group and want a snack. Whether it is at dinner time or after a game, ordering in is a popular custom.

 B. Read the questions aloud with a partner. Then listen to the conversation between Gaby, Philip, and Marc, and answer the questions.

1. What do the students want to do?

   _____

2. What kinds of food do they talk about ordering?

   _____

3. How much money does Philip have?

   _____

4. Why do they decide against ordering Chinese food?

   _____

5. Why does Gaby want to order pizza?

_____

6. When does the restaurant give its customers free pizza?

_____

7. What kind of pizza do they consider first?

_____

8. What does Gaby not like to have on her pizza and why?

_____

9. What will be the total cost of the pizza?

_____

10. Why does Gaby suggest that they tell the pizza restaurant not to hurry?

_____

C. Use these expressions to replace the idioms in bold. Write out the sentences using the expressions.

   a) Hey guys.
   b) I'm starving.
   c) five bucks
   d) What will it come to?
   e) It took ages.
   f) all-dressed
   g) hold the mushrooms
   h) take your time
   i) plus a tip
   j) money on me

1. I'm not in a hurry today, so you can **go slowly**. We can get together later in the day.
2. I'd like a pizza **with everything on it**, please, but **don't put on any mushrooms**.
3. I took the bus to school this morning, and there was a big traffic jam. **It took a long time** to get here.
4. I don't have **a lot of money in my pocket** today. Can you lend me **five dollars**?
5. **Listen everyone, I'm really hungry.** Let's order in.
6. **How much will it cost?**
7. The food will come to $15, **and we have to add money for a tip**.

Turn to page 35 for Exercise D.

Ordering Supper

A. Work in pairs. Pretend that you want to order supper together, and you each have $7 to spend. Decide what kind of food and drinks you want.

B. Write a dialogue. Discuss what you are going to order and the price. Use some of the idioms from page 30.

Granola

A. Discuss these questions.

1. What kind of food do you like to eat for snacks?
2. What kinds of foods are good for you?
3. Can you name some foods that are considered "health foods"?
4. What is granola? Do you know anyone who likes to eat it?

B. Read the story and answer the questions that follow.

Granola

Do you consider yourself a "granola" type? How about your parents? You may know the term but you probably don't know the history of granola. In our society, granola has become a cultural icon. Today, people who eat granola are sometimes called "health-food freaks." They are the same people who eat tofu and bean sprouts. In fact, granola has more often been associated with counterculture. For many years it was considered "anti-establishment" to eat granola.

How did a food consisting of grains, nuts, coconut oil, dried fruit, and sprinkled with brown (as opposed to white) sugar gain this reputation? Granola was first made popular by hippies in the 1960s and it seemed revolutionary at that time, but in fact it was invented in the 1860s. It was the brain-child of Dr. Jackson, who put his patients on a strict anti-meat diet. He decided to create a nutritious food for them to eat. He baked thin sheets of graham flour, which were moistened and crumbled into bits. Then they were baked again into rock-hard nuggets, called granula. They were served with milk. Dr. Jackson advertised his product widely, and it became the first processed health food sold in America. It also became the first breakfast cereal.

A few years later Dr. Jackson's idea was copied by John Harvey Kellogg, who added some ingredients such as cornmeal and oats, and began marketing his own "granula." When Dr. Jackson found out about this new product, he sued Kellogg. Kellogg then changed the name of his product to granola.

For a while, granola was forgotten, but it resurfaced in the 1960s as an all-in-one, nutritious meal that was dry and portable. It was advertised as the perfect food for vagabonds and hippies living on the street or in communes. It fact, people called it the perfect food for anyone "too stoned to cook." It was even recommended for revolutionaries because it could be made in big enough quantities to feed an army and it didn't spoil easily. It was particularly useful when they staged sit-ins and demonstrations or occupied buildings for any length of time.

Because granola became the symbol of the hippie movement, many people ridiculed it as unappetizing and unappealing. But, by the 1970s, people who believed natural products were good for their health began to buy it. Later, it began to sell in supermarkets. Today, we have granola bars which are often loaded with sugar or honey, and coated with chocolate. A survey in *Glamour* magazine investigated how healthful granola bars are. They found that they are approximately as nutritious, and as fattening, as the average candy bar. Take your pick!

Questions

1. What do "health-food freaks" eat besides granola?
2. What reputation did granola have in the past?
3. What is granola made of?
4. Why did Dr. Jackson create granola?
5. How was granola made?
6. How did Dr. Jackson make his product popular?
7. How was Kellogg's product different?
8. What was Jackson's reaction to Kellogg's product?
9. Name four advantages of granola.
10. Where were people expected to eat granola?
11. Give two reasons why granola was recommended for revolutionaries.
12. Name two situations in which revolutionaries found granola useful.
13. What association made granola unappetizing to many people?
14. Who began to buy granola in the 1970s?
15. How do granola bars compare with candy bars?

Grammar Close-Up: Requesting Permission

Using "Can," "Could," and "May" to Request Permission

Use **could** and **may** to make polite requests for permission to do something. **Can** is less formal and is generally used with family and friends.

Put requests in question form with the modal (**can**, **could**, or **may**) at the beginning of the sentence. Use the base form of the main verb.

> EXAMPLES: May I use your telephone?
> Can we come in now?
> Could I borrow your pen?

 Requests for permission cannot be made with the second person **you** form.

> EXAMPLE: ✗ May you come in?

can I	could I	may I
can you	could you	✗
can he	could he	may he
can she go?	could she go?	may she go?
can we	could we	may we
can you	could you	✗
can they	could they	may they

Find the errors and correct them. Check (✔) sentences that are correct.

1. Can he comes with us tomorrow?
2. Could she join the team next year?
3. May you come in now?
4. Can she borrows your umbrella?
5. May I please be excused?
6. Can we leaves the classroom?
7. Could I smoke a cigarette here?
8. May you open the door please?
9. Can we to come in now?
10. Could I join you for lunch?

"Would," "Could," or "Can" for Polite Requests

Use **would**, **could**, or **can** with **you** to make a polite request that someone do something for you. The polite request form **would**, **could**, or **can** is often accompanied by the word **please** before the main verb.

> EXAMPLES: Would you (please) pass me the butter?
> Could you (please) tell me the time?
> Can you (please) answer the phone?

 It is possible to use **could** or **can** with different pronouns (first, second, third person) to make polite requests. It is not possible to use the first or third person pronouns to make polite requests with **would**.

> EXAMPLE: ✔ Could I borrow ten dollars?
> ✗ Would I borrow ten dollars?

Choose the correct sentence.

1. a) Excuse me, could you please tell me the time?
   b) Excuse me, should you please tell me the time?

2. a) Can you show me where to get the bus downtown?
   b) Are you show me where to get the bus downtown?

3. a) Would we leave now or do we have to wait for something?
   b) Could we leave now or do we have to wait for something?

4. a) I can't hear you. May you please speak louder?
   b) I can't hear you. Can you please speak louder?

5. a) Can we have a wake-up call for eight o'clock please?
   b) Would we have a wake-up call for eight o'clock please?

6. a) Could you please repeat that question?
   b) Should you please repeat that question?

7. a) Would everyone please stop talking immediately?
   b) May everyone please stop talking immediately?

8. a) Can you please give me your homework next class?
   b) Should you please give me your homework next class?

9. a) May you please come to class on time in future?
   b) Would you please come to class on time in future?

10. a) Could I ask you for some help with this problem?
    b) Would I ask you for some help with this problem?

Going Abroad: Pizza Pie

A. Choose the best words to complete the story.

"Pizza" is the Italian **1** _____ for pie. This popular
                (idea, custom, word, dessert)

fast food comes **2** _____ Naples in the south of Italy. Pizza is
          (to, from, at, of)

made from a **3** _____ bread crust with toppings
     (flat, tall, expensive, sweet)

that **4** _____ added. Most pizza toppings start with oil and
   (are, is, be, will)

tomato paste. Then other **5** _____ such as
           (toppings, vegetables, meats, cheese)

peppers, onions, mushrooms, and pepperoni are added. Finally,

6 _____ is added and the pizza is baked in the
(oil, cheese, crust, salt)

7 _____ until the cheese melts.
(pot, kitchen, oven, table)

One reason **8**_____ love pizza is the taste. A pizza
(kids, child, people, adults)

9_____ bread, vegetables, meat, and cheese so
(cooks, contains, has, sells)

10_____ is also really very nutritious. There are many
(it, that, one, another)

ways to eat pizza. Some people **11**_____ it with a knife
(buy, eat, order, make)

and fork, but most people prefer to pick up slices and eat them with

12_____ hands.
(their, his, our, its)

B. Discuss these questions.

1. What is your favourite kind of pizza?
2. How often do you eat pizza?
3. Where do you usually eat it?
4. Do you use your hands or a fork?

Let's Order In

D. Listen to the conversation and write the missing words.

Philip: Hey guys, I'm starving. Let's _____ in.

Marc: Yes. That's a great idea Philip. I'm hungry too.

Gaby: What shall we order: pizza, Chinese food, chicken?

Philip: I _____ Chinese food but I only have five
bucks on me. What will _____ come to?

Marc: That depends _____ what we order. What
_____ you think Gaby?

Gaby: I think we should get pizza. Last time we ordered
Chinese food. It _____ really good but it
took ages. Pizza always comes fast.

Philip: OK, _____ get pizza. What's _____
place called, the one where you get the pizza free if it
takes more _____ half an hour?

Marc: Free pizza. Great.

Gaby: Not free, Marc. Not unless it takes more than
_____ an hour.

Marc: Well pizza's good anyway. What kind should _____
order?

Philip: _____ about all-dressed?

Gaby: All-dressed is good _____ I don't like mushrooms. I _____ the texture. Ask for all-dressed without mushrooms.

Marc: OK. I'll order one large pizza, all-dressed, hold the mushrooms. How much _____ it cost?

Philip: _____ 12 bucks I think. That comes to four dollars each, plus a tip. I think we _____ enough. I'll tell the pizza place to hurry.

Gaby: No, don't tell _____ to hurry. If it takes them more than half an _____, the pizza is free.

Marc: Yes, Philip. Tell them to _____ their time!

E. Practise the dialogue with a partner.

Your Finances

Where Does Your Money Go?
Interaction
Vocabulary

Money in the Bank
Reading: Scanning

Opening a Bank Account
Listening Activity 4

To Work or Not to Work...
Discussion
Writing

Saying Numbers: Thousands
Number Practice

Grammar Close-Up
WH-Question Words

Going Abroad
Money Makes the World Go Around
Vocabulary

Never Trust a Stranger
Listening Activity 5
Episode 1: Making Plans

Where Does Your Money Go?

A. Work with a partner. Check (✔) the correct category for each expense.

	Rent and utilities	Clothing	Books and school supplies	Entertainment	Transportation	Personal expenses
a dictionary						
a bus pass						
shampoo						
a hydro bill						
a school jacket						
renting a video						
a present for a friend						
art supplies						
cigarettes						
auto insurance						
winter boots						
a meal in a restaurant						
a loaf of bread						
a parking ticket						
a calculator						
a pair of jeans						
gasoline						
a ruler						
a dry-cleaning bill						
parking fees						
tights						
gym shorts						
a bathing suit						
sneakers						

	Rent and utilities	Clothing	Books and school supplies	Entertainment	Transportation	Personal expenses
residence fees						
cable TV						
a meal in the cafeteria						
a lottery ticket						
toothpaste						
a car tune up						
a book of love poems						
a basketball game						
a new belt						
computer discs						
a toothbrush						
laundry detergent						
the monthly phone bill						
writing paper						
loose-leaf paper						
a quart of milk						
a stapler						
a school bag						
lipstick						
aspirin						
a rock concert						
a movie						
service charges at the bank						
a library fine						
text books						
binders						
laundromat charges						
postage stamps						
a passport photo						
disco entrance fees						

B. Work with a partner. Put a star (*) beside the things that either or both of you have had as expenses this year.

Money in the Bank

A. Work in pairs. Match the term with the definition.

1. a piece of paper you use to pay a bill   a) balance
2. to take money out of the bank   b) deposit
3. an account where you save money   c) interest
4. the money you keep in your account   d) withdraw
5. to put money into the bank   e) savings account
6. extra money the bank pays on your savings   f) cheque
7. money you pay for bank services   g) bank book
8. a book that shows your transactions   h) chequing account
9. a list of deposits and withdrawals that you   i) statement
   receive from the bank every month   j) service charge
10. an account that lets you write cheques

B. Look at the questions. Then scan the text to find the answers.

1. What are two reasons to keep your money in the bank?
2. How can you withdraw money after the bank is closed?
3. What is another use of a bank card?
4. What is a savings account for?
5. What is one advantage of a savings account?
6. How do you keep track of your savings account?
7. How often is interest paid?
8. How is a chequing account useful?
9. What are two small disadvantages of a chequing account?
10. How can you keep track of your chequing account balance?

Money in the Bank

Keeping your money in the bank is a good idea. Your money is safe and you also make interest. Interest is the extra money the bank pays you for leaving your money there. With today's technology, you can use your account even if the bank is closed. You can use a bank card that gives you access to a banking machine. A bank card also lets you pay at the cash register in a store by debiting your account directly at the point of purchase.

You can choose from several different kinds of bank accounts. It is important to select the account that is best for you. A savings account is a good place to put money that you don't need to spend right away. It also gives you the most interest. When you open a savings account, the bank gives you a bank book with your account number on it. When you withdraw or deposit money, the transaction will be marked in your bank book. Usually interest is calculated at the end of each month, but some savings accounts pay daily interest.

A chequing account lets you write cheques, and it is useful for paying regular expenses such as rent and telephone or hydro bills. The cheques you use usually have your name and address on them. They also have your account number. You have to pay a small amount, called a service charge, each time you write a cheque. A chequing account pays some interest, but it is less than you get from a savings account. With a chequing account, you get a statement every month. The statement tells you how much money has gone into and out of your account during the month. It lets you keep track of the balance in your account.

Opening a Bank Account

Listening Activity 4

A. Read the questions aloud with a partner. Then listen and answer the questions.

1. What is the student going to study?

   _____

2. What happened to the bank account the student used to have?

   _____

3. What kind of account does the student ask about first?

   _____

4. What kind of account does the teller suggest?

   _____

5. Who can open a student account?

   _____

6. What are two advantages of a student account?

_____

7. What is a third advantage?

_____

8. What are two uses of a bank card?

_____

9. What does the student decide to do?

_____

10. When does the teller say she can use the account?

_____

Turn to page 48 for Exercise B.

To Work or Not to Work...

A. Discuss these questions.

1. What do you spend your money on?
2. What regular expenses do you have?
3. Why do you think so many students work part time?
4. Have you worked or do you plan to work during the summer?
5. Do you currently have a part-time job?
6. What are some good part-time jobs for students?
7. What are some disadvantages of part-time jobs for students?

B. Write two paragraphs. Give your ideas about students who work.

Saying Numbers: Thousands

Partner A

Read the numbers on the left to your partner. Then write the numbers that your partner reads to you.

Partner B: Turn to page 47.

96,837	_____
43,102	_____
434,411	_____
139,004	_____
86,310	_____

Now change roles. Write the numbers that your partner reads to you. Then read the numbers on the right to your partner.

_____	548,909
_____	577,454
_____	120,541
_____	18,987
_____	326,097

Grammar Close-Up: WH-Question Words

Use WH-question words when you want specific information. Put the WH-question word before the auxiliary verb at the beginning of the sentence. Look at the chart to see the kind of information given by each WH-question word.

WH-word	Kind of information	Example
when	time	When do you want to meet? At three o'clock.
where	location	Where are you going? To my next class.
what	description	What is he doing? He's skating.
why	explanation	Why do you feel tired? Because I went to bed late.
who	identity	Who is talking? Mike is.
which	choice	Which one do you want? I want the blue one.
how	manner	How do you get good marks? I study hard.

A. Match the questions and the answers.

1. Who is asking the questions?   a) by bus
2. Why are they sitting in that room?   b) chemistry
3. Where do they study English?   c) He's sleeping on the desk.
4. How does she get to class?   d) The teacher is.
5. When do we have an exam?   e) They are waiting for class to start.
6. What is that student doing?   f) at college
7. Which course do we have next?   g) on Monday

B. Read the paragraphs and answer the questions with complete sentences.

Karen is a student in a college downtown. She usually leaves for school early. She likes to arrive early. When she is late, she doesn't have time to drink coffee and read the paper before she has class. Karen begins school at 8:30.

Other people in Karen's class have coffee at home and arrive later. Fred sometimes arrives in a bad mood because he has trouble finding a place to park his car. He often has to park several blocks away and walk to the college. Karen is happy that she lives near the subway and that she doesn't need to worry about parking. Melanie and Tina live near the college so they can walk to class.

Questions

1. Where does Karen study?
2. Why does she usually leave for school early?
3. When doesn't she have time for coffee?
4. When does she like to read the newspaper?
5. What time does Karen begin class?
6. Why does Fred sometimes arrive in a bad mood?
7. Where does he often have to park?
8. Where does Karen live?
9. Why is Karen happy about where she lives?
10. How do Melanie and Tina come to college?

Going Abroad:
Money Makes the World Go Around

Use the words below to complete the paragraphs on page 45.

valuable   drink   money   spend   things   metal   advantage
common   trade   beads   objects   coloured   tea

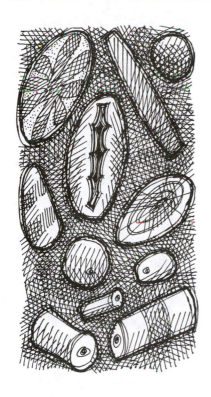

A long time ago, people didn't have **1**_____. They traded objects to get what they wanted. This worked pretty well for a long time, but sometimes people couldn't agree on a **2**_____, so they started using special **3**_____ just for trade. This was the beginning of money.

Many different **4**_____ were used as objects of trade. For example, in ancient Egypt, salt was important, so people traded blocks of salt. In ancient China, tools were very important, so people made small **5**_____ tools and traded them.

In some countries, the tokens were not **6**_____ things. They were **7**_____ objects. In Africa people traded stones and **8**_____. Aboriginal peoples in Canada used **9**_____ beads and shells. In other places, people traded whales teeth, feathers, and even **10**_____ leaves. Using tea leaves had an **11**_____, too. If you didn't **12**_____ your money, you could always pour hot water on it and **13**_____ it!

Never Trust a Stranger

Listening Activity 5

Episode 1: Making Plans

A. Look at a map of the world and locate the following places:

Hong Kong, Jakarta (Indonesia), Montreal, Trois-Rivières, Vancouver, Victoria

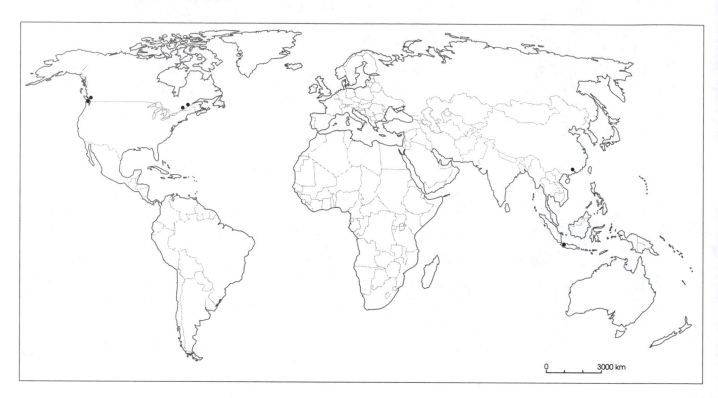

 B. Read the questions aloud with a partner. Then listen and answer the questions.

1. Where is Brantford College located?

   _____

2. Why does Julie live in residence at her college?

   _____

3. What is Julie discussing with her roommate?

   _____

4. What exams do Julie and Megan have?

   _____

5. Why are Julie's parents in Indonesia?

   _____

6. How long does it take to get from Vancouver to Jakarta?

   _____

7. Who is Julie going to travel with?

   _____

8. Why does Julie have a good accent in French class?

   _____

9. Who lives in Trois-Rivières?

   _____

10. What does Marc do?

    _____

11. What is Lisa like?

    _____

12. Why do Megan and Julie have to stop talking?

    _____

C. Work in pairs. Take turns telling the story.

D. Write a summary of the story.

Saying Numbers: Thousands

Partner B

Write the numbers that your partner reads to you. Then read the
numbers on the right to your partner.

_____	576,032
_____	345,010
_____	82,435
_____	14,358
_____	77,890

Now change roles. Read the numbers on the left to your partner.
Then write the numbers that your partner reads.

456,897	_____
28,411	_____
47,023	_____
16,981	_____
88,309	_____

Opening a Bank Account

B. Listen to the dialogue and write in the missing words.

Teller: Good afternoon. Can I help you?

Customer: Hello. Yes, I'd _____ to open a new
                account.

Teller: _____ you already have an account with us?

Customer: No, I've just moved _____ from out of town.
                I'm going to be studying business administration
                _____ Ahuntsic College.

Teller: _____ you have an account with another
                bank in _____ home town?

Customer: Yes, but I closed _____ before I moved
                here. I'd like to open a Savings Account. By the way,
                _____ I write cheques on a Savings
                Account?

Teller: Do _____ know about special student
                accounts?

Customer: No, I don't.

Teller: There are several advantages. I could explain
                _____ the student accounts work if you
                like.

Customer: Sure. If there _____ advantages I'm
                definitely interested.

Teller: If you are a student in _____ post-secondary
                institution—that is, at a college or university, you can
                have _____ account with no service charges.

Customer: Do I need _____ have a minimum balance?

Teller: There is no minimum balance and you don't
                _____ to pay monthly charges either.

Customer: Can _____ write cheques?

Teller: Yes, you can _____ there is no charge for
                cheques.

Customer: What about a bank card for the automatic teller?

Teller: Yes, you _____ have a bank card. It's good
                for the automatic teller and it's good for debit trans-
                actions at the point of purchase.

Customer: You've convinced me. I'd like _____ open a student account.

Teller: OK. Just fill _____ this form and we'll open your account today.

Customer: Thanks for _____ help.

C. Work in pairs. Practise the dialogue with your partner.

D. Work with your partner. Write a new dialogue about banking transactions.

The Weather Wherever You Go

The Weather Quiz
Interaction
Reading

Are You Winter Wise?
Vocabulary

Clearing the Snow in Montreal
Listening Activity 6

Grammar Close-Up
Simple Past Tense

In the Past
Grammar Game

Going Abroad
The Rainiest Place on Earth
Vocabulary

Never Trust a Stranger
Listening Activity 7
Episode 2: Dorval Airport

The Weather Quiz

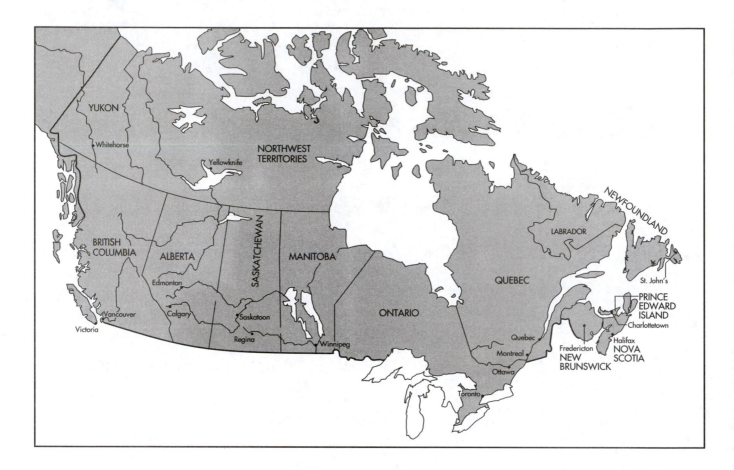

A. Read the paragraph. Then close your book and write as your teacher dictates.

Canada is famous for being a cold country with low temperatures and a lot of snow. But many people outside Canada don't realize that Canada has very hot weather in the summer. Even in winter there are some surprises in the weather patterns of different regions of the country. How much do you know about Canada's weather?

B. Work with a partner to choose the best answers to the quiz.

1. The highest temperature ever recorded in Canada was:
   a) 38 degrees
   b) 34 degrees
   c) 45 degrees

2. The city with the mildest climate is:
   a) Quebec City
   b) Winnipeg
   c) Victoria

3. Which months have the worst snow storms?
   a) December and January
   b) January and February
   c) December and March

4. The coldest capital city in the world is:
   a) Reykjavik, Iceland
   b) Ottawa, Canada
   c) Ulan Bator, Mongolia

5. The coldest temperature ever recorded in the northern hemisphere was:
   a) –38 degrees
   b) –78 degrees
   c) –68 degrees

6. What causes the temperature to drop the lowest?
   a) blizzards
   b) wind chill
   c) night

7. The most dangerous weather phenomenon in Canada is:
   a) avalanches
   b) cold
   c) lightning

8. The biggest hail stones to fall in Canada were the size of:
   a) tennis balls
   b) peas
   c) golf balls

9. Which city has the most snow and wind but one of the mildest winters?
   a) Halifax
   b) St. John's
   c) Saskatoon

10. July 11 is called "Canadian weather day." Why?
    a) It has the most rain.
    b) It has the most wind.
    c) It has the most surprises.

11. Which Canadian city has the most rain?
    a) Victoria
    b) Vancouver
    c) St. John's

12. Which region of Canada has the most snow?
    a) eastern Canada
    b) the Arctic
    c) the Prairies

C. When you have finished, turn to page 64 and check your answers.

Are You Winter Wise?

Look at the picture on page 54. Work with a partner. Find:

1. something to help a car start in winter
2. two ways to clear the sidewalk
3. a tree with needles
4. a place where birds can eat
5. two ways to clear the windshield of a car
6. a part of a house that is not heated
7. a tree without leaves
8. two things we use on ice so we won't slip
9. something we have to change on our car at the beginning and end of winter
10. two things we wear on our hands to keep warm

Clearing the Snow in Montreal

Listening Activity 6

A. Complete the paragraphs with the words below.

**cost   sidewalks   streets   equipment   snowfall   budget
pedestrians   snow   centimetres   vehicles   crew   trucks**

Montreal is a snowy city. The annual __1_____ can be as much as 300 __2_____, This creates a big problem for traffic and for __3_____ who have to walk on the sidewalks. If the snow weren't cleared, cars and __4_____ couldn't pass in the __5_____ and people would be in danger of falling on the slippery __6_____.

The City of Montreal operates a giant fleet of snow removal __7_____ and a large __8_____ of workers to keep the streets clear. Because of the heavy snowfall, Montreal has a snow-clearing __9_____ of $60 million annually. That is the __10_____ of maintaining all the __11_____ and of employing the hundreds of people who work to keep the streets free of __12_____ in winter.

Every day, throughout the world, 44 000 thunderstorms occur. There are around 100 lightning flashes every second!

B. Match the pictures to the sentences on page 57.

1. Giant snowplows push the snow to the side of the street.
2. Snow tractors clear the sidewalks of snow.
3. Tow-trucks tow cars and leave them many blocks away.
4. Workers put up "No Parking" signs along the street.
5. Trucks drive away and dump the snow in the river.
6. Trucks pass to scatter sand and salt on the streets.
7. Snowblowers suck up snow and shoot it into trucks.

 C. While you listen, put the pictures in the correct order.

Grammar Close-Up: Simple Past Tense

Use the simple past tense for actions completed in past time.

> EXAMPLE: I **watched** a movie last night.

The regular form of the simple past tense is formed by adding **ed** to the base form of the verb.

> EXAMPLE: I walk   I walk**ed**

Some verbs require spelling changes before the **ed** is added. See the chart in Appendix 2, page 174.

Many common everyday verbs are irregular in the affirmative form of the simple past tense. See Appendix 3, page 175.

A. Match the base form and past tense form in the affirmative.

1. live	a) told	10. put	j) put
2. take	b) climbed	11. give	k) brought
3. eat	c) ran	12. say	l) lived
4. run	d) gave	13. know	m) ate
5. climb	e) saw	14. tell	n) came
6. throw	f) went	15. come	o) took
7. meet	g) threw	16. find	p) met
8. go	h) found	17. see	q) knew
9. bring	i) got	18. get	r) said

B. Read the story. Put the verbs in the simple past tense.

The Apple Tree

When we were young, we __1_____
(live) in the country. My brother and I
__2_____ (go) to school together
every day. We often __3_____
(meet) our friends along the road. We
__4_____ (take) our time. We
__5_____ (hunt) rabbits and looked
for fruit trees. The road to the school
__6_____ (run) past a farmer's
fields.

One fall day we __7_____ (get) into
trouble with a farmer. We __8_____
(find) an apple tree. When we
__9_____ (see) the juicy red apples,
my friend __10_____ (climb) the tree. He picked apples and
__11_____ (throw) them down. I __12_____ (catch)
the apples and we all __13_____ (eat) a lot. The farmer
__14_____ (see) us eating his apples and was very angry.

We __15_____ (bring) a nice red apple to the teacher. My
brother __16_____ (put) the apple on the teacher's desk.
When she __17_____ (see) the apple, she said "Thank you."
Nobody __18_____ (tell) her where the apple
__19_____ (come) from.

Negative Form

Regular and irregular past tense verbs form the negative in the
same way. The auxiliary verb **did** signals past time and **not** signals
negation. The main verb is in the base form with both irregular and
irregular verbs.

EXAMPLES: I walked. I did not **walk**.
       I went. I did not **go**.

The contraction of **did not** is **didn't**.

The sunniest place on earth is the eastern Sahara
Desert. It has sunshine 97 percent of the time.

A. Match the base form and the irregular affirmative form of the past tense.

1. leave		a) rode
2. sit		b) rang
3. drive		c) wore
4. stand		d) got off
5. sing		e) made
6. make		f) saw
7. wear		g) drove
8. speak		h) left
9. know		i) waited
10. get off		j) stood
11. ride		k) heard
12. see		l) knew
13. hear		m) sang
14. ring		n) spoke
15. wait		o) sat

B. Put the sentences in the negative form. Use the contraction.

EXAMPLE: The bus left early. **The bus didn't leave early.**

1. The bus driver drove dangerously.
2. The passengers sat at the front of the bus.
3. The driver knew all the passengers.
4. We sang songs during the bus ride.
5. He saw a person running after the bus.
6. The driver spoke to the man behind him.
7. They waited in the rain for half an hour.
8. You rode your bicycle to work every day last year.
9. We heard the siren of a police car.
10. The driver wore a uniform with a hat.
11. She rang the bell three times.
12. The old lady stood for the whole ride.
13. The driver had an accident.
14. We left before the five o'clock rush hour.
15. We got off at the same bus stop.

Question Form

Use the simple past tense to ask questions about events that were completed in past time.

EXAMPLE: Did you finish all your homework yesterday?

Signal past time by using **did** before the subject of the sentence. Use the base form of the main verb.

EXAMPLE: You ate breakfast early. **Did** you **eat** breakfast early?

A. Match the base form and the irregular present simple form of the verbs.

1. read   a) drank
2. feel   b) left
3. leave   c) took
4. win   d) had
5. pay   e) woke up
6. take   f) tried
7. spend   g) spent
8. drink   h) said
9. eat   i) ate
10. have   j) won
11. try   k) read
12. wake up   l) paid
13. say   m) felt

B. Read the story about Ben's summer in Paris. Then make questions with the verbs that are in bold type.

Ben Taylor was very lucky. He **entered** a contest and **won** a trip to Paris. Ben **spent** last summer in Paris. He **loved** his morning routine. He usually **woke up** early because he liked to have time for breakfast. He **went** to a cafe near his hotel for breakfast. He usually **had** coffee and croissants. Ben always **sat** on the terrace of the cafe. He **ordered** coffee and **read** the newspaper. After he finished his coffee Ben **paid** the bill and left the restaurant.

EXAMPLE: What did Ben enter?

1. What _____?
2. Where _____?
3. What _____?
4. Why _____?
5. Where _____?
6. What _____?
7. Where _____?
8. What _____?
9. What _____?
10. When _____?

In the Past

This is a guessing game, to find out about what people in the class did in the past.

A. On a piece of paper, write down three unusual things about yourself from the past. Write one thing that you really did and two things that are false.

B. One student begins by reading his or her list to the group. People in the group try to guess which one thing is true by asking questions. The student answering the questions should try to make it as difficult as possible for them to guess.

The person who guesses correctly is the winner. That student then reads his or her list, and continues the game.

Going Abroad: The Rainiest Place on Earth

A. Discuss these questions.

1. Can you think of any places that are very dry?
2. Name some places that receive a lot of rain.
3. What could make the weather in a region change?

B. Work with a partner. Read the paragraphs and choose the correct words.

We all know that some <u>   1   </u> are famous for
(countries, places, streets)

their rain—for example, Singapore and Tahiti in the rainy season

or London, England, and Vancouver, B.C., almost any time of the

<u> 2 </u> . In the mountains of northeastern India, near
(day, week, year)

Bangladesh, there <u> 3 </u> a town with an incredible
(are, have, is)

<u> 4 </u> of rain. The name of the town is Cherrapunji.
(history, picture, story)

For many years Cherrapunji was known as the wettest town on

earth. It rained four days out of five every year, <u> 5 </u> 250
(then, with, about)

days a year. People <u> 6 </u> to market in the rain, children
(go, went, came)

played in the rain, farmers worked in the rain. Cherrapunji had the

7 _____ rainfall ever recorded **8** _____ :
(youngest, loudest, heaviest)   (here, there, anywhere)

2 647 centimetres of rain in the year 1861. The average rainfall in

London or Vancouver by comparison is only 63 centimetres

9 _____ a year.
(from, in, of)

Yet, surprisingly, the region that has **10** _____ the rainiest
(been, was, had)

place in the **11** _____ is now facing a water shortage, and
(sky, city, world)

even the possibility of drought. The reason **12** _____ deforest-
(be, was, is)

ation. When trees are cut down, there is little soil left to hold the

water. The water cycle is broken and the annual rainfall decreases

sharply. As a result, Cherrapunji **13** _____ facing a water short-
(has, are, is)

age. The **14** _____ town in the world may soon be the
(oldest, wettest, driest)

driest!

Never Trust a Stranger

Listening Activity 7

Episode 2: Dorval Airport

A. Work in pairs and see what you remember about the last episode. Answer the questions orally.

1. Where does Julie Gregg live?
2. Where are her parents?
3. Who are her cousins?
4. What does Marc do?
5. How old is he?
6. How old is Lisa?
7. What are their plans?

B. Read the questions aloud with a partner. Then listen and answer the questions.

1. Why are Marc and Lisa late?

   _____

2. How much time do they have before their plane leaves?

   _____

3. What two things do they have to do when they arrive at the airport?

   _____

4. How many times will they be changing planes on the trip?

   _____

5. How much does the taxi cost?

   _____

6. What did Lisa forget in the taxi?

   _____

7. What is the temperature in Indonesia?

   _____

8. What two things does the Air Canada ticket agent give them?

   _____

9. What is their flight number?

   _____

10. How long is the flight to Vancouver?

    _____

11. Where are they going to meet Julie?

    _____

12. What airline are they taking?

    _____

C. Work in pairs. Close your books and tell each other everything you can remember about the story.

D. Write a summary of the story.

The Weather Quiz

Read and check your answers from the quiz on page 52.

1. Canada is a country with extreme differences in temperature from winter to summer. It is surprising that a country with temperatures that are often –30 degrees in winter can be extremely hot in summer. The highest recorded temperature was in Yellow Grass, Saskatchewan, where it rose to 45 degrees Celsius.

2. Quebec City is known for its humid climate which makes both winter cold and summer heat feel more uncomfortable. Winnipeg has a dry climate but also has extreme temperatures. Victoria has cool summers and warm winters. It is so mild that it rarely snows there.

3. We have snow storms all winter, but the worst ones occur in the months of December and March. This is because, in these months, cold Arctic air meets warmer air from the south. When the two systems meet, it can mean heavy snow. In January and February, we are usually in a period of cold air.

4. Iceland has a cold name but, in fact, it has a higher temperature than New York because of the Gulf Stream that comes from the Gulf of Mexico. Ottawa is pretty cold but it is not nearly as cold as Ulan Bator, Mongolia.

5. The northern regions of North America and Scandinavia have recorded many low temperatures but the coldest temperature ever recorded in the northern hemisphere was in Siberia. Thermometers recorded an incredible –68 degrees.

6. We all know that temperatures drop lower at night. We also know that a winter blizzard with blowing snow can be bitterly cold, but the biggest cause of very low temperatures is neither night nor blizzards. It is what scientists call the wind-chill factor.

7. Avalanches can suddenly crash down mountainsides and sweep away everything in their paths. Lightning is a summer phenomenon that can strike suddenly and be deadly as well. But extreme cold is more dangerous to people in Canada than avalanches and lightning combined.

8. Hail is always a problem for farmers on the Canadian prairies, and the hail stones can be very large. The record for the largest hailstones was set in 1984 in Manitoba, when hail stones as big as golf balls fell on farmers' crops.

9. This city is the foggiest, snowiest, wettest, windiest, and cloudiest in Canada. It has the most days with wet weather and freezing rain in Canada, yet the people who live here like their climate. They say it builds character. The city is St. John's, Newfoundland, and strangely enough, it has one of the mildest winters, ranking third after Victoria and Vancouver.

10. In the history of Canadian weather, two days are special. October 2 is special because is has had no surprises. It is the most unexciting weather day of the year. July 11 is called Canadian Weather Day because more surprising weather events have happened on this day than on any other. July 11 has had floods, tornadoes, storms, and mud slides.

11. St. John's, on the east coast, has the most extreme weather conditions in Canada, but the rainiest part of the country is the west coast. Vancouver is the wettest city with 63 cm of rain per year. Victoria is protected by the Olympic Mountains and has a much drier climate than Vancouver.

12. The Canadian Arctic has very cold temperatures but, surprisingly, it has very little snowfall. Like the Prairies, the Arctic is a very dry region that is closer to desert than other parts of Canada. Eastern Canada receives far more snow annually than either of the other two regions.

5

What's Happening to Our Environment?

Trees We Eat
Vocabulary

Forests of the World
Scanning for Information

The Sloth
Listening Activity 8

Hero of the Rainforest
Reading: Scanning
Interaction

Grammar Close-Up
Past Continuous Tense

Grammar Close-Up
Adverbs with Question Words **How** and **Why**

Going Abroad
Preserving Trees Around the World
Scanning for Information

Never Trust a Stranger
Listening Activity 9
Episode 3: Meeting Julie

Trees We Eat

A. Work in pairs. Look at the list of things people eat. Classify them according to whether they come from a tree, a vine, or a plant.

	Tree	Vine	Plant
pineapples			
lemons			
cinnamon			
sugar			
chewing gum			
strawberries			
tea			
maple syrup			
chocolate			
grapefruits			
pecans			
peaches			
grapes			
coconuts			
bananas			
peas			
basil			
cantaloupe			
pumpkins			
lettuce			
apples			

B. Use these words to complete the paragraph.

grapefruits   dessert   almonds   spices   coffee   nuts
sweetener   wonderful   morning   fruits

Why do we need trees? Well, what would you do without your
__1_____ cup of __2_____? What about your
favourite chocolate __3_____? Coffee and chocolate come
from trees. We also get some wonderful __4_____ such as
cinnamon and nutmeg from trees. All of our __5_____
such as walnuts, __6_____, and coconuts grow on trees.
Without trees we would have few __7_____. Apples,
pears, oranges, and __8_____ come from trees. So does
our favourite __9_____, maple syrup. What would we do
without all the __10_____ things that come from trees?

Forests of the World

Work with a partner. Look at the maps and charts on pages 70 and
71. Find the answers to these questions.

1. Name three kinds of forests.
2. Which provinces in Canada provide the most wood?
3. Which three countries have the most wood removed each year?
4. Name five things in the house that are made from wood.
5. Name five forest products that can we eat.
6. Which kind of forests gives us "Christmas trees"?
7. Which kinds of forests are found in Canada?
8. Name three forest products that we use in the classroom.
9. Name two forest products that help us smell good.
10. What is the leading cause of jungle destruction?
11. What are most of the trees cut down in Canada used for?
12. Where is more than one-third of the world's newsprint
     produced?
13. Name a chemical product made from wood that is used in
     photography.
14. Name three areas of the world that have tropical rainforests.
15. How many jobs does the forestry industry provide in Canada?

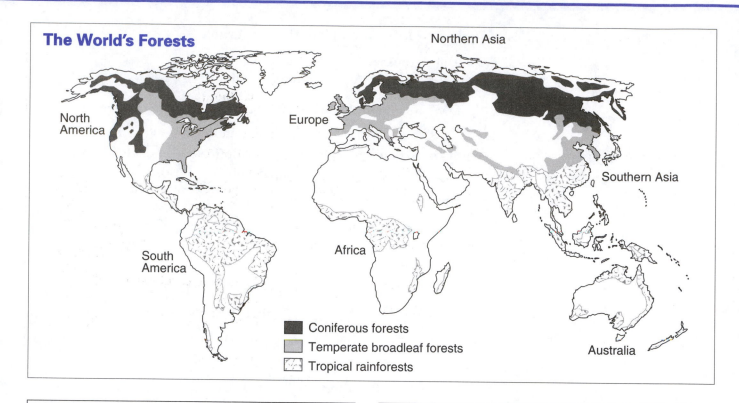

The World's Forests

- Coniferous forests
- Temperate broadleaf forests
- Tropical rainforests

Leading countries in forest products	Wood removed from forests in one year
Indonesia	149 010 000 m³
Canada	171 310 000 m³
Brazil	225 910 000 m³
India	245 030 000 m³
China	263 370 000 m³
United States	335 700 000 m³

Leading provinces for forest products in Canada	Wood removed from forests in one year
Ontario	28 130 000 m³
Quebec	36 520 000 m³
British Columbia	74 560 000 m³

Causes of destruction of jungles, 1960–1990

Other

Population increase, colonization

Ranching, plantation farming

Logging

Total jungle loss, 1960-1990

100%
90
80
70
60
50
40
30
20
10
0

temperate broadleaf forest

coniferous forest

tropical rainforest

Forest Products

Wood Products

Lumber
flooring
furniture
musical instruments
pencils
window frames
boats
boxes
doors
fences
bowling pins
baseball bats
chopsticks

Plywood
boats
airplanes
containers
furniture
house foundations

Round timber
utility poles
bridges
fence posts
log homes

Fibre Products

Hardboard
garage doors
furniture
cabinets
signs
automobile interiors

Paper and cardboard
paper
books
boxes
newspaper
bags
tissue paper
packaging

Chemical Products

film
turpentine
plastics
tool handles
printing inks
animal feeds
disinfectants

Fuel Products

charcoal
fireplace logs
sawdust

Other Forest Products

Bark
cork
dyes
fuel

Sap
maple sugar
maple syrup

Fruit and seeds
pine nuts
pecans
black walnuts
cranberries
blueberries

Leaves
household cleaners
soap
perfumes
medicines

Canadian Facts

- Forestry is one of the biggest industries in Canada, and provides more than a million jobs.
- Ontario, British Columbia, and Quebec are the biggest wood-producing provinces.
- Canada exports more forest products than any other country in the world.
- Two-thirds of trees cut down in Canada each year are made into pulp and paper.
- Canada produces 40 percent of world's supply of newsprint—mostly for export.
- British Columbia produces most of Canada's lumber—mostly for export.
- Christmas trees and maple syrup are other important forest products.

The Sloth

Listening Activity 8

A. Discuss these questions.

1. Can you think of any animals that are lazy?
2. Name some animals that live in trees.
3. Are there any animals that sleep in trees?

B. Listen to information about an animal called the sloth. Check (✔) the subjects that are mentioned on the tape.

1. different names for the sloth
2. the animal's size
3. sleep and movement
4. where the animal lives
5. why people like the sloth
6. how it escapes predators
7. its fur
8. how it communicates
9. how it swims
10. the climate it likes

C. Read the questions aloud with a partner. Then listen and answer the questions.

1. Name three languages in which the word for the sloth means "lazy."

_____

2. How many hours per day is a sloth awake?

_____

3. How fast does a sloth generally move?

_____

4. What is the usual position for a sloth?

_____

5. What special trick can a sloth do with its head?

_____

6. How many teeth does a sloth have?

_____

7. Name two ways in which a sloth protects itself from enemies.

_____

8. How does a sloth's fur grow?

   _____

9. What colour does a sloth's fur become because of the wet climate?

   _____

10. In which part of the world do sloths live?

    _____

Hero of the Rainforest

A. Discuss these questions.

1. What is a rainforest?
2. Where can we find rainforests?
3. Name some plants and animals that live in rainforests.
4. What is the problem concerning rainforests today?

B. Work in pairs. Scan the text for answers to these questions. Discuss the answers orally. Do not write.

1. How many kinds of trees can you find in an area of 10 square kilometres of rainforest?
2. How many kinds of insects can there be on one tree?
3. How do trees contribute to the rain cycle?
4. What do rubber tappers do?
5. What is causing the destruction of the rainforest?
6. What kind of people are affected by the destruction of the rainforest?
7. How did Chico Mendes earn his living?
8. Who did Chico Mendes protest against?
9. Explain the conflict between Chico Mendes and Darli Alves da Silva.
10. What happened to Chico Mendes?
11. What happened to Darli Alves da Silva?

Hero of the Rainforest

Enter a tropical rainforest and you will find a dark and mysterious world, rich with plant and animal life. Scientists estimate that a typical area of 10 square kilometres of rainforest can have 750 different kinds of trees, 125 kinds of mammals, 400 kinds of birds, and 100 types of reptile. One tree alone can have 400 different kinds of insects!

The rainforest of the Amazon basin is an essential part of the Earth's ecosystem. The trees that grow there release moisture into the air, contributing to the rain cycle. The trees also prevent soil erosion. The rainforest is a vast ecological system that provides food, medicines, and economic activity for many people, including rubber tappers. Rubber tappers are people who harvest latex, the liquid from rubber trees.

Unfortunately, in recent times there has been massive destruction of forested areas. Developers have put the Amazon rainforest in danger by clearing land for cattle ranching, and by building roads for logging and mining activities. This type of development has also endangered the way of life of the people who depend on the forest for their survival. One man who decided to fight back against the destruction of the forest was a rubber tapper named Chico Mendes.

Chico Mendes made his living by tapping latex from the rubber trees and selling it. His way of life depended on the Amazon rainforest. Chico Mendes began to lead protests against the ranchers who were clearing land for farming, and against the miners and loggers who were destroying the forest. One of the ranchers who wanted to cut the trees on the rubber tappers' land was Darli Alves da Silva. Mendes led a group of 200 people who turned da Silva back.

Several days later, Mendes was shot and killed as he was leaving his house. Da Silva and two of his sons were arrested for the crime. They were convicted of murder and sent to jail. Chico Mendes will be remembered as a courageous man who helped the world realize the dangers of destroying the Amazon rainforest.

C. Read the text carefully and write answers to the questions you discussed.

Grammar Close-Up: Past Continuous Tense

Use the past continuous for past actions that were temporary.

> EXAMPLES: It was raining hard yesterday.
> Jacqueline was wearing a raincoat.

Use the **ing** form of the main verb to show continuous aspect. Use the past tense of the auxiliary verb **be** to show that the action took place in past time.

To form the negative, add **not** after the auxiliary verb **be**.

> EXAMPLES: It wasn't raining yesterday.
> People weren't wearing raincoats.

Affirmative		**Negative Form**		**Negative Contraction**	
I was		I was not		I wasn't	
you were		you were not		you weren't	
he was		he was not		he wasn't	
she was		she was not		she wasn't	
it was	wearing	it was not	wearing	it wasn't	wearing
we were		we were not		we weren't	
you were		you were not		you weren't	
they were		they were not		they weren't	

Use the auxiliary **was** for singular forms and **were** for plural forms. The exception is **you** singular. Use **were** as the auxiliary with **you** singular.

Write these sentences in the negative. Use the contraction.

1. Tom was asking for directions.
2. Anne was carrying a newspaper.
3. Jean was working in a restaurant.
4. Sylvain and Bob were going to the bank.
5. We were sitting in the back of the bus.
6. Lili was speaking to me.
7. Max was waiting for us in the cafeteria.
8. Robert was looking for Nadia.
9. They were meeting after class.
10. Pierre was studying Spanish.

Questions with the Past Continuous

Use the auxiliary verb **be** to ask questions. Put the auxiliary verb before the subject.

> EXAMPLE: Was he wearing a red sweater yesterday?

was I
were you
was he
was she
was it   wearing?
were we
were you
were they

Grammar Close-Up: Adverbs with Question Words "How" and "Why"

Use **how** to ask questions about manner (about how an action happened). Put **how** before the auxiliary verb.

> EXAMPLE: How was he driving the car? **Slowly.**

Use **why** to ask questions about cause (the reason an action happened). Put **why** before the auxiliary verb. The answer to a **why** question usually begins with the word **because**.

> EXAMPLE: Why was he driving **fast?** Because he was late for work.

A. Match questions and answers.

1. How was the teacher speaking?
   a) hungrily
   b) suddenly
   c) clearly

2. How were they playing their music?
   a) loudly
   b) luckily
   c) clearly

3. How was Anne smiling?
   a) luckily
   b) happily
   c) loudly

4. How was the person sleeping?
   a) quietly
   b) hungrily
   c) fast

5. How were your students listening?
   a) carefully
   b) nicely
   c) loudly

6. How was it raining?
   a) well
   b) hard
   c) nervously

7. How was the bus moving?
   a) good
   b) fast
   c) nice

8. How were Nicole and Paul eating?
   a) badly
   b) hungrily
   c) sleepily

B. Match the questions and answers.

1. Why was Mario walking quickly?
2. Why were Robert and Lucie smiling?
3. Why was Tom shouting?
4. Why was Steve making a sandwich?
5. Why were Nadine and Helen late?
6. Why were they drinking water?
7. Why was Daniel sleeping?
8. Why was Suzanne crying?

a) because he was tired
b) because he was angry
c) because they missed the bus
d) because they were happy
e) because he was late
f) because she was sad
g) because they were thirsty
h) because he was hungry

C. Choose the correct form of the word.

1. Anne was having a (quiet / quietly) sleep.
2. The bus was moving (slow / slowly).
3. They were playing music (loud / loudly) at the party.
4. Max was playing tennis (bad / badly) yesterday.
5. Please be (quiet / quietly). I'm reading.
6. It was raining (hard / hardly) this morning.
7. I can speak English (good / well) now.
8. The baby was smiling (nice / nicely).
9. The bus left (late / lately) this morning.
10. It was a (good / well) supper.

Going Abroad:
Preserving Trees Around the World

Scan page 78 for answers to these questions.

1. What do trees do for us?
2. What kind of products should we avoid?
3. Why should we buy Brazil nuts?
4. What kind of woods should we buy?
5. Why should we avoid corned beef?
6. How can we avoid buying beef from rainforest land?
7. What rule should we follow when we walk in a forest?
8. Why should we support the World Wildlife Fund?
9. How can we save on wasteful gift wrapping?
10. How can we take care of trees around us?

Plant a tree!

Trees gives us shade, provide homes and food for animals, and are beautiful to look at, too.

Preserving Trees Around the World

Shopping Power

- Buy Brazil nuts and cashews, which come from living tropical trees, and support people making their living from the forest.
- Choose products made from local woods such as pine, maple, or cherry.
- Avoid buying products made from teak, mahogany, or rose-wood, which come from tropical rainforests
- Avoid disposable paper products such as paper cups and plates.
- buy paper products such as writing paper and envelopes that are made from recycled paper.
- Try not to buy beef from rain-forest land. (Try to find out from fast food chains where they buy their beef.)
- Try to avoid corned beef and canned beef, as these are often rainforest products.
- When walking in the forest, follow the rule "Take nothing but pictures, leave nothing but footprints."
- Support the World Wildlife Fund, which uses donations to buy rain-forest land and preserve it.

At Home

- Reuse large envelopes that arrive at your home. Just put a new address label on (any piece of paper will do), and send the envelope out again.
- Save giftwrap and reuse it. Ribbons and string can also be reused. Another idea is to wrap gifts with newspaper. Comics are especially fun.
- Use rags (worn-out clothes) instead of paper towels for cleaning.

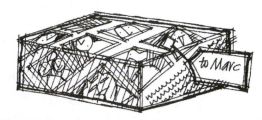

Be a Green Helper

- Recycle paper, especially news-paper.
- Start a paper-recycling program at your school or workplace.
- Take care of the trees around you: water them.

Never Trust a Stranger

Listening Activity 9

Episode 3: Meeting Julie

A. These are some of the things Marc and Lisa have to do when they get to the airport. Put the steps in the correct order.

a) clear security

b) board the plane

c) listen for their flight to be called

d) get a boarding pass

e) give the agent their tickets

B. Read the questions aloud with a partner. Then listen and answer the questions.

1. What time does Marc and Lisa's flight arrive in Vancouver?

_____

2. What does the airline ticket agent tell them?

_____

3. What two things does the ticket agent ask them to give him?

_____

4. Where does Lisa have her passport?

_____

5. What happens when she tries to take it out?

_____

6. Who helps Lisa pick up her things?

_____

7. Why did Julie check in before her cousins arrived?

_____

8. Why does Julie ask if they want coffee?

_____

9. What does Lisa ask Julie about her parent's house?

_____

10. What does Marc want to do in Hong Kong if they have time?

_____

11. Why do they have to wake up early in Hong Kong?

_____

12. What is their flight number?

_____

C. Work in pairs. Take turns telling the story.

D. Write a summary of the story.

6

Sports in Our Lives

Sports Talk
Puzzle
Vocabulary

The Y
Reading

Joining the Y
Listening Activity 10

Grammar Close-Up
Gerunds

Sports Presentation
Oral Report

A Sport I Like
Writing

Going Abroad
Spin Doctors
Vocabulary

Never Trust a Stranger
Listening Activity 11
Episode 4: Paul Hawke

Sports Talk

Work in pairs. Use the clues to complete the puzzle.

Across

4. People often use a lot of equipment to do this indoor sport.
6. Football and hockey players wear this on their heads for protection.
8. We do this sport in a boat. We can do it alone or with partners. We use oars to move the boat.
9. We play this team sport outside in summer, with a bat and a ball.
10. We do many sports outside on the grass. This area is called a playing _____.
11. This team sport is the most popular in the world.
12. People go into a pool or lake this way. Some people like to do this from high up. Others like to do it close to the water.
13. We play this sport with a partner or in a group of four. We use a ball and rackets.
17. This is an American sport that is played in the fall. It is a popular college sport.
18. People do this sport in winter, in the mountains.
20. The best season for playing hockey and skating is _____.
21. Some people like to swim in lakes or rivers. Others prefer to swim in a _____.
22. We play tennis with a ball and a _____.
23. A _____ is a good form of transportation, and is a great way to get exercise.
25. People play hockey or skate indoors or outdoors in a _____.
26. Two people do this sport in a ring. They wear heavy gloves.

Down

1. _____ is something people do for exercise or to compete in races.
2. This sport builds muscles. Strong people do it in competitions.
3. The best season for swimming outdoors is _____
5. People do this sport on water. They do it in a boat. The wind moves the boat.
7. We play this team sport with a ball in a gym or on the beach.
9. In this game, people throw balls through baskets on a court.
14. People do this popular summer sport in pools, lakes, or oceans.
15. This winter sport is played on ice with a stick and a puck.
16. People do this sport on lakes and rivers, in a boat. They use a paddle.
19. This sport is done outside, with a club and a small white ball.
20. People play this sport in the water. They use a ball.
24. Some people like to do this kind of exercise in parks. Others do it on city streets.

The Y

A. Discuss these questions.

1. What do the letters YMCA and YWCA stand for?
2. What are some activities you can do at the Y?
3. Who can join the Y? Are there age restrictions?

B. Read the text quickly for information that will help you answer True (**T**) or False (**F**) to the following statements.

1. The Y restricts its membership to certain groups.
2. The Y began in downtown Montreal.
3. The Y is like a cheap hotel.
4. You can probably practise karate at the Y.
5. The Y has summer camps for children.
6. You can learn how to fix your car at the Y.

The Y

Who in North America doesn't know about the Y? The name is short for YMCA, which stands for Young Men's Christian Association, but that really doesn't tell the story today. The Y isn't only for young people. It has residences, community activities, and sports programs for people of all ages. The M isn't only for men. There is the YWCA with residences and sports programs for women. The C isn't only for Christian. The Y has members of every race and religion. It is non-denominational. There is even the YMHA/YWHA (where the H stands for Hebrew). The A isn't only for Association. It is for swimming pools, summer camps, leadership programs, and adult education.

The YMCA began in London, England in 1844. The YWCA began in 1855. Both organizations are very successful today, and have members from many different backgrounds. The founder of the Y was a man named George Williams. The downtown campus of Concordia University in Montreal is named after him.

The Y is probably best known for its residences. People travelling on a slim budget know they can always stay at the Y. You can find a Y in nearly every city in Canada and the United States and the residences are clean, safe, friendly, and cheap.

The Y is also well known for its sports programs. Its buildings have good sports facilities such as gyms and swimming pools. There are many different sports programs where people can learn everything from swimming to self-defence. People go to the Y after school or after work to lift weights, do aerobics, swim, play basketball, or maybe go jogging on the roof of the building.

Some of the most popular summer camps belong to the Y, too. Campers go to the country where they can swim, canoe, and learn about nature. Many people have good memories of sitting around a campfire singing and making new friends through the Y.

The local Y is an important part of many communities. You can take computer courses that are not very expensive, learn to speak a new language, find out how to repair a car, or take a course in public speaking. It provides many new services for our changing world.

C. Read carefully and answer the questions.

1. What do the letters YMCA stand for?
2. What religion are members of the Y?
3. How many years passed between the founding of the YMCA and the founding of the YWCA?
4. What is "Sir George Williams"?
5. Why are the Y residences popular?
6. When do people go to the Y for sports activities?
7. Where do people jog at the Y?
8. Name five things children can do at summer camp.
9. What is an advantage of computer courses at the Y?
10. Name three kinds of courses you can take at the Y.

Joining the Y

Listening Activity 10

A. Read the questions aloud with a partner. Then listen to the conversation and answer the questions.

1. What kind of course does the caller ask about?

   _____

2. When is the advanced class?

   _____

3. Why is the caller unsure of which class to take?

   _____

4. Why did she have to drop the course before?

   _____

5. Why does the woman encourage her to try the advanced class?

   _____

6. When does the next session start?

   _____

7. Who can use the weight-training equipment?

   _____

8. What is Mike's job?

   _____

9. Who can help the caller get started on the equipment?

   _____

Turn to page 91 for Exercise B.

Grammar Close-Up: Gerunds

A gerund is made from a verb but it functions as a noun. A gerund can function as the subject or object of a sentence. It can also function as the object of a preposition.

Examples:

Subject: **Swimming** is good for you.
Object: We like **swimming**.
Object of a preposition: He is interested in **swimming**.

A gerund is made with the present participle form of the verb (**ing** form without the auxiliary verb **be**). Look at the examples of a noun and a gerund.

Noun: **Cigarettes** are bad for you.
Gerund: **Smoking** is bad for you.

The verb **go** + gerund is often used to describe sports and activities. Examples are **go camping**, **go skiing**, **go dancing**, **go jogging**, **go shopping**.

A. Underline the subject in each sentence. Match the subjects to the gerunds.

1. Books give interesting information.	a) lying down
2. Exercise is good for people.	b) drawing
3. Humour makes people laugh.	c) swimming
4. Cigarettes are dangerous.	d) reading
5. Weights build strong muscles.	e) bodybuilding
6. Silence is golden.	f) dancing
7. Ballet develops the muscles.	g) keeping quiet
8. Art develops the mind.	h) smoking
9. Rest helps relax the body.	i) telling jokes
10. TV can be educational for children.	j) watching TV

B. Replace the noun **something** with a gerund form of the verb.

**lie   exercise   smoke   walk   overeat   do   camp
raise   swim   jog**

1. Something children is an important responsibility.
2. Something causes people to gain weight.
3. Many people are afraid of something in the ocean.
4. They don't like something because of the mosquitos.
5. Something alone at night can be dangerous in a big city.
6. Something exercise can be very good for your health.
7. Doctors advise against cigarettes and something.
8. Something in the sun can cause skin cancer.
9. A good way to get exercise in the park is something.
10. Something daily is a good way to stay fit.

C. Complete the sentences with the correct prepositions before the gerunds.

from to of about for before at in after over

1. Let's have coffee _____ going to class.
2. Are you interested _____ seeing a movie on Friday?
3. How _____ going for dinner after the movie?
4. We are thinking _____ inviting Anne to join us.
5. Thank you very much _____ giving us a lift home.
6. Marc is pretty good _____ fixing a computer.
7. We are looking forward _____ seeing you again soon.
8. We can go to the restaurant _____ parking the car.
9. We are tired _____ skiing all weekend.
10. They chose tennis _____ playing soccer.

Sports Presentation

Prepare a five-minute presentation about a sport you know. Give information about the following points:

Part A

1. What is the sport?
2. Do you play it yourself?
3. How long have you played it?
4. Where do you play it?
5. How often do you play it?
6. What season do you play it in?
7. How long did it take you to learn it?

Part B

1. What are the rules?
2. What special clothing or equipment is needed to play?
3. Are any special skills needed?

Part C

1. What risks are involved?
2. How long does it take to become proficient?
3. What benefits do you get from playing this sport?
4. To whom would you recommend this sport?

A Sport I Like

Write about a sport you like. Use the ideas above to help you.

Going Abroad: Spin Doctors

Work with a partner. Read the paragraphs and choose the best words.

In South America, roller-blading is the rage. There they have roller-blading paths in parks and ovals where we have ice-skating rinks. The **1**_____ do
(athletes, players, students)
every variation on skating that you can imagine:
roller-hockey, artistic roller skating with pairs,
dance and figures, and road-racing.

It is **2**_____ for people from North
(easy, difficult, fun)
America to compete with the South Americans
because our **3**_____ are too short
(winters, summers, legs)
here. People from Argentina and Colombia
practise all year long.

The race is very exciting. Athletes wear skin-tight suits and bike

4_____ , and move around the rink at top speed.
(helmets, paths, shirts)
Meanwhile, the fans stomp, whistle, cheer, sing, boo, and

5_____ objects such as full coke bottles **6**_____ the
(carry, put, throw)   (in, onto, to)
track. Of course, this brings **7**_____ action to a stop—until the
(my, your, the)
next **8**_____ , that is.
(race, skater, team)

Never Trust a Stranger

Listening Activity 11

Episode 4: Paul Hawke

A. Read the passage quickly. Then close your book and write as the teacher dictates.

Hong Kong is a very busy economic centre situated on the south-east coast of China. Its name means "fragrant harbour." It is one of the main gates of entry for passengers arriving in Asia from North America. Passengers often stay overnight in the city before they continue to their destinations in other parts of Asia.

B. Read the questions aloud with a partner. Then listen and answer the questions.

1. What does Lisa forget in her hotel room?

   _____

2. What does Marc remind Lisa about?

   _____

3. How long do they have to wait in the airport in Hong Kong?

   _____

4. How do they meet Paul Hawke?

   _____

5. What do Julie and Lisa think about Paul Hawke?

   _____

6. What information does Marc give Paul in the plane?

   _____

7. What kind of business is Paul Hawke in?

   _____

8. How long do the cousins plan to be in Indonesia?

   _____

9. What is Borobudur?

   _____

10. What is the temple near?

    _____

11. Which one of the cousins has a camera?

    _____

12. What does Marc remind Lisa about as they leave the plane?

    _____

C. Work in pairs. Tell each other everything you can remember about the story.

D. Write a summary of the story on a sheet of paper.

Joining the Y

B. Listen to the conversation and write the misssing words.

YMCA: Hello. Downtown Y. Can I help you?

Caller: Hi. _____ like some information about your programs, please.

YMCA: Sure. What would you like _____ know?

Caller: Well, my friend and I would like to know if you have aerobic dance classes.

YMCA: Yes. We have beginners' class on Tuesday and Thursday afternoons, and there's also _____ advanced class on Monday and Wednesday evenings.

Caller: Is the advanced class really hard? I'm not a beginner, but I don't know if I'm advanced either.

YMCA: Well, I'd say it _____ challenging. Have you taken a class before?

Caller: Yes, about a year ago, but I had to drop _____ because I was too busy at school. Now I want to try again.

YMCA: Look, why don't you try it and see how it goes? If you find it difficult, you can always change to the easier class. The instructor is really great, though. The class is _____ lot of fun.

Caller: OK, I guess I'll give it a try. When does the next session start?

YMCA: A week from Monday, the 19th.

Caller: Great. Oh, I wanted _____ know about weight-training. Do you have facilities, and you do have instruction?

YMCA: We do have a well-equipped gym. You _____ use it as often as you like with a membership. There's no formal instruction, but there's a guy named Mike who is in charge of the equipment. He's always willing to help someone out the first few times.

Caller: Can he show me how the equipment works and every-thing? I really want to start on a weight-training program, but I'm not sure how _____ begin.

YMCA: Oh, I'm sure Mike can help you out. Why don't you come down _____ look around?

Caller: That's a good idea. I think I'll come _____ tomorrow. Maybe _____ bring a couple of my friends.

C. Practise the dialogue with a partner.

D. Write a new dialogue about joining the Y.

Fads and Fashions

What Do We Wear?
Puzzle
Vocabulary

Blue Jeans
Reading

The Mystery of Bruce Lee
Listening Activity 12

Grammar Close-Up
Present Perfect Aspect (1)
Duration of Time

Going Abroad
Entertainment Around the World
Vocabulary

Never Trust a Stranger
Listening Activity 13
Episode 5: A Surprise Call

What Do We Wear?

Use the clues to complete the puzzle.

Across

2. People wear these on their feet in summer.
3. We wear these to sleep at night.
4. You wear these on your hands in winter. They have five fingers.
7. These are on your feet. They are made of cotton or wool.
8. Men and women exchange these when they get married.
10. People wear these to go swimming
12. T-shirts and jeans are made from this material. It comes from a plant.
13. People of all ages wear these pants, but they are most popular with teenagers.
16. A man wears this around his neck when he wears a suit.
17. This material is used to make sweaters and coats. It comes from sheep.

18. Before this kind of machine was invented, people had to sew clothes by hand.
20. This invention makes getting dressed easier and faster.
21. You use these to tie your sneakers.

Down

1. This wonderful invention helps people see better if they don't want to wear glasses.
5. This beautiful fabric comes from an animal. It is often used to make blouses.
6. Sometimes women wear this above the knee. Other times they wear it long.
9. Many women wear this on their lips. It comes in shades of pink and red.
10. These round objects help us close our shirts.
11. We used to wear these shoes just for sports, but now we wear them all the time.
14. You have a left one and a right one. You wear these on your feet.
15. You wear this around your waist, to hold up your pants.
18. You wear this around your neck in winter.
19. You wear these to keep your hands warm. They have a thumb, but no fingers.

 Blue Jeans

A. Discuss these questions.

1. How many people in the class are wearing jeans today?
2. How often do you wear blue jeans?
3. How many pairs of jeans do you own?
4. Why do you think that blue jeans are so popular?
5. Do your parents ever wear jeans?
6. What brand of jeans is the most popular?
7. What brand of jeans is the most expensive?
8. What are some places where you can't wear jeans?

B. Skim the first sentence of each paragraph and see which paragraphs talk about the following topics.

1. the word "jeans"
2. the invention of jeans
3. counterfeit jeans
4. how jeans became popular
5. the status of jeans today

Blue Jeans

A. Fashions come and fashions go, but blue jeans stay. Blue jeans are probably the only item of clothing that is more popular today than when it was invented 150 years ago. Jeans are so much a part of our culture that they are defined in the dictionary, displayed in museums, and sought after all over the world. Everyone from babies to grandmothers wears jeans, although the biggest consumers are certainly teens. Every year new looks for jeans appear in the fashion ads and new variations appear in the streets. Jeans come in different colours and they are worn ripped, faded, and patched.

B. What a surprise it would be for the inventor of jeans to see them as fashion items for the general public! When Levi Strauss invented jeans, he thought he was making work pants for miners. Levi Strauss was a tent maker from Germany who hoped to make a fortune selling tents to workers in the gold mines of California. He soon saw a bigger need, however. The miners were always tearing their pants and he had the idea of making heavy cotton pants. His pants had double stitching and copper rivets to make them stronger.

C. Strauss modelled his pants on the ones worn by sailors in the port of Genoa in Italy. This is the origin of the word "jeans." He soon switched from using tent canvas for the pants to another fabric called by the French name "serge de Nimes." When California miners tried to say this name, they pronounced it "denim" which is what the fabric is still called today. Strauss's first customers loved jeans because they were practical, comfortable, and durable. Today, people love jeans for the same reasons. They are easy to wash, they mould to the owner's shape, and they last forever.

D. Jeans weren't always popular with the general public. For years jeans were considered to be work pants. During the First World War, 24 million pairs of jeans were sold as work pants for American soldiers, for example. But things changed radically in the 1960s thanks to two events. In 1963, *Newsweek* magazine invented the term "teenager" and put a picture of a teenage girl wearing jeans on its cover. After that, movie stars and singers such as James Dean, Marilyn Monroe, and Elvis began to adopt the look. Soon jeans had become a major fad.

E. With this popularity, of course, came problems. Counterfeit jeans began to appear on the market. Popular brands like Levis, which were famous for their quality and creative advertising, soon had copiers using their labels. First in Italy, then in the Far East and Latin America, people began to produce illegal copies of brand-name jeans. Sometimes the copies were easy to spot because they looked strange or had spelling mistakes in the labels. Other times the copies were closer to the original. Levi Strauss has a big security department whose job is tracking down the fakers. The company estimates that no factory can produce fake Levis for more than two months before it is discovered. But to be safe, it may be better to check the spelling on the label of your jeans—just to make sure that they won't fall apart in the wash.

C. Read the text carefully and answer the questions.

1. What shows that jeans are an important part of our culture?
2. With whom are jeans most popular?
3. What are some varieties of jeans that are found in popular culture?
4. How were jeans first invented?
5. What were two special characteristics of Levi Strauss's first jeans?
6. Where did Levi Strauss get the first model for jeans?
7. Where did the word "denim" originate?
8. What do people today love about jeans?
9. What did people think of jeans at the beginning of the twentieth century?
10. What suddenly made them popular with the general public?
11. Name two ways to spot counterfeit jeans.
12. What steps does the Levi Strauss Company take to stop counterfeiters?

The Mystery of Bruce Lee

Listening Activity 12

A. Discuss these questions.

1. Who was Bruce Lee?
2. What was he famous for?
3. What happened to him?

 B. First read the questions aloud with a partner. Then listen and answer the questions.

1. What kind of movies did Bruce Lee make?

   _____

2. How old was he when he died?

   _____

3. When and where was Bruce Lee born?

   _____

4. What did he want to become an expert in?

   _____

5. Describe Bruce Lee's version of kung fu.

   _____

6. What did Bruce Lee do in Hollywood?

   _____

7. What happened on May 10, 1973?

   _____

8. What happened over the next few weeks?

   _____

9. What did Lee do when he had a headache?

   _____

10. What happened afterwards?

    _____

11. Give examples to show that Lee was in good physical condition.

    _____

12. What did some people suggest as the reason for Lee's sudden death?

    _____

13. What was the title of his final film?

    _____

C. Write the story of Bruce Lee. Give as many details as you can from the listening.

Grammar Close-Up: Present Perfect Aspect (1)

For Duration of Time

Use the present perfect aspect to suggest duration of time. Use it to focus on an action or state that started in the past and continues in the present. It is used in contrast to the simple past tense which is used when an action began and ended in past time.

EXAMPLES: Do you live in Paris?
No, we lived in Paris for three years, but we don't live there now.
Simple past: The action was completed in past time.

Yes, we have lived in Paris for six years. (and we still do)
Present perfect: The action began in the past and continues in the present.

Use the auxiliary verb **have** and the past participle of the main verb to form the present perfect.

EXAMPLE: She has lived in Paris for three years.

Verbs that occur in the present perfect for duration of time have both regular and irregular past participle forms. The regular form of the past participle is the same as the simple past tense (add **ed**).

Base form	Past tense	Past participle
be	was, were	been
go	went	gone (to school)
have	had	had
know	knew	known
live	lived	lived
speak	spoke	spoken (a language)
work	worked	worked

See Appendix 3, pages 175-176 for a full list of irregular past participle forms.

A. Complete the sentences with the present perfect form of one of the verbs listed above.

1. The Smiths and the Tremblays _____ neighbours for 15 years.

2. Min Hee _____ English since she spent her summer vacation in Toronto.

3. Alex and Carla _____ in the same office since the company opened.

4. Max and I _____ to the same school since we were in grade three.

5. Jacques _____ the head librarian at the college for six years.

6. Mrs. Gregory _____ in the house next door since I was a child.

7. The Smith family next door _____ the same car for many years.

8. Daniel _____ in an engineering office ever since he graduated university.

9. Lise _____ Steve since elementary school.

10. Francine _____ to the same language school since last year.

B. Choose the simple past or present perfect form of the verb.

1. Marianne (was/has been) in Japan from 1990 to 1992.
2. Michel (worked/has worked) there since 10 years ago.
3. Karen (lived/has lived) in Toronto all her life.
4. Sam (was/has been) to London on business in March.
5. He (lived/has lived) next door to us since he was a boy.
6. Jane (had/has had) a cold since last weekend.
7. I (knew/have known) those people since 1986.
8. Maria (worked/has worked) in Jakarta in 1987.
9. Jack (spoke/has spoken) Turkish when I met him.
10. Bob (was/has been) a student here since last September.

C. Write the correct form of the verb for each sentence.

1. Jane Green _____ (live) in the apartment next door before she got married.
2. Robert White _____ (live) in Houston since he got a job with the oil company.
3. My friend Simon _____ (speak) Japanese since he worked in Japan as an English teacher.
4. Elizabeth _____ (speak) French to the travel agent in Switzerland.
5. Patrick McCarthy _____ (be) a teacher at this college for about three years now.
6. Michel _____ (be) a police officer since he graduated from college last year.
7. Susanna _____ (be) a lawyer before she became my business partner.
8. John _____ (know) Dr. Han since they played in the same orchestra.
9. Carolyn _____ (know) my uncle when they were students at the same college.
10. No one on the team _____ (have) an accident this year.

Present Perfect Questions Related to Duration of Time

When questions use the present perfect to refer to duration of time, the expression **long** or **how long** is often used.

 Long does not refer to distance, but to time, here.

EXAMPLES: Have you been here long? no, just ten minutes
How long have you lived in Seattle? (for) five years

Read the sentences. Write questions to help you get more information. Use **how long** and the present perfect.

EXAMPLE: André is a student. How long has André been a student?

1. André lives in Montreal.
2. He goes to a technical college.
3. André's uncle and aunt have a grocery store.
4. André works in the store on weekends.
5. He knows a girl from Quebec.
6. They are in the same classes.
7. She speaks French.
8. Her family lives in Quebec.
9. She works in the library after school.
10. André and the girl are good friends.

Going Abroad: Entertainment Around the World

Use the words below to complete the paragraphs.

**music   world   video   centuries   power   societies
dancing   halls   entertainment   programs   screen**

Who among us doesn't like to be entertained? The world of entertainment is the world of excitement. Throughout the **1**_____, traditions of dance, **2**_____, and theatre have developed in different ways in different places. When you think about it, all **3**_____ have contributed to the wonderful **4**_____ of entertainment. Shadow puppets, opera, flamenco **5**_____, and rock and roll come from different places. Each society has its own rhythms and stories and art forms. But all of them have the **6**_____ to thrill people from other places, too.

In recent times movies, television and **7**_____ have made it possible for millions of people to see the same **8**_____. Entertainment, from the flaming arrow that opened the Olympic Games in Lillehammer to the Rolling Stones in Concert in New York, is as near as the television **9**_____. Yet still people continue to sit in circus tents, concert **10**_____, and theatres to take part in the special thrill of live **11**_____.

Never Trust a Stranger

Listening Activity 13

Episode 5: A Surprise Call

A. Look at the tourist brochures and answer the questions on page 104.

The Temple of Borobudur was built in the eighth century. It is a very famous example of Buddhist art. Many figures carved in stone decorate the temple walls. For many years, the temple was lost in the jungle, but in 1976, work began to restore it. Borobudur was opened to the public in 1983.

The central part of the Temple of Borobudur is 40 metres above the ground. The temple walls extend for a length of 6 kilometres, and contain many masterpieces of Buddhist art. Visitors to Borobudur should plan on spending the day there to see this fascinating monument.

Borobudur is located about 45 kilometres northwest of the city of Yogyakarta. Visitors can travel to the temple by taxi or by public bus. Public transportation is available at the bus terminal or in front of some hotels. Buses stop before they reach the temple and visitors have to walk the rest of the way.

1. What is Borobudur?
2. What decorates the temple walls?
3. How long did it take to restore the temple?
4. How far do the walls extend?
5. Why are the walls fascinating?
6. How can visitors travel to the temple?
7. Why do visitors have to walk before they reach the temple?

 B. Read the questions aloud with a partner. Then listen and answer the questions.

1. What is the family discussing after dinner?
   _____

2. How did Paul Hawke know how to reach Marc?
   _____

3. Why is Paul going to Yogya?
   _____

4. What does he suggest to Marc?
   _____

5. When will they go to Yogya?
   _____

6. What does Lisa want to see when they get to Yogya?
   _____

7. Why does Julie think Paul will be a great guide?
   _____

8. Why is Julie looking forward to the trip?
   _____

9. Who will make the hotel arrangements?
   _____

10. How will the cousins pay?
    _____

11. What does their uncle suggest they can find in Yogya?
    _____

12. What does Marc think Lisa can buy?
    _____

C. Close your book. Then tell your partner everything you can remember about the story.

D. Write a summary of the story on a sheet of paper.

Technology

8

Machines and Inventions
Word Scramble

Technology Quiz
Interaction

Chester Carlson's Marvellous Machine
Listening Activity 14

Grammar Close-Up
Present Perfect Aspect (2)
Indefinite Past Time

Can Robots Think?
Reading

Numbers and Words
Vocabulary

Going Abroad
Capturing the Moments
Vocabulary

Never Trust a Stranger
Listening Activity 15
Episode 6: Ticket to the Temple

Machines and Inventions

These words are related to different kinds of technology. Put the words into categories. You should have six groups of three words each.

---

neon   **compact disk**   **monitor**   **cord**   **receiver**   **steering wheel**
X-ray   **brakes**   **fluorescent**   **keyboard**   **cassette**   **dial**   **CAT-scan**
printer   **record**   **exhaust pipe**   **tungsten**   **ultrasound**

Technology Quiz

Discuss the questions with a partner. Then choose the best answers.

1. A modem is used to:
   a) start a car engine
   b) send information between computers
   c) send signals to a satellite

2. A holograph is:
   a) a shiny picture
   b) a three-dimensional picture
   c) an instant picture

3. Which of these is not part of a car?
   a) a battery
   b) a clutch
   c) a ribbon

4. The first black and white television service was in:
   a) England
   b) the United States
   c) Germany

5. In order to receive E-mail, you need to have:
   a) an enamel receiver
   b) a computer terminal
   c) a touch-tone phone

6. The Lumiere brothers were the inventors of
   a) the electric light
   b) the first cinema
   c) the movie camera

7. A silicone chip is:
   a) a kind of food
   b) found on the beach
   c) used in computers

8. Alexander Graham Bell invented the telephone while:
   a) teaching in London, England
   b) vacationing in Nova Scotia
   c) working in New Jersey

9. The first human being to go into space was:
   a) French
   b) American
   c) Russian

10. Which person invented the most objects in his lifetime?
    a) Thomas Edison
    b) Leonardo da Vinci
    c) F. Braun

11. Which person did not invent a camera?
    a) J. Hamilton
    b) E. Land
    c) G. Eastman

12. The first video tape system for home use came from:
    a) Korea
    b) the United States
    c) Japan

13. In 1971, Intel Corporation introduced the first:
    a) pocket calculators
    b) mini cassette players
    c) wireless radio

14. Skyscrapers were built because of the invention of:
    a) escalators
    b) stairs
    c) elevators

Chester Carlson's Marvellous Machine

Listening Activity 14

A. Discuss these questions.

1. What are some machines that we use every day?
2. What are some machines that are used in offices?

B. Read the questions aloud with your partner to check vocabulary. Then listen and answer the questions.

1. When and where did Chester Carlson work?

   _____

2. What was Chester Carlson's job?

   _____

3. What happened when Carlson experimented with sulphur?

   _____

4. What deal did the Haloid company make with Carlson?

   _____

5. Why was the first copier not very practical?

   _____

6. What happened if the paper didn't move fast enough through the machine?

_____

7. What did the first machines come equipped with?

_____

8. How much did the first copier weigh?

_____

9. Why was the weight a problem?

_____

10. How did the Haloid company show how easy it was to use the machine?

_____

11. How much did the Haloid company's sales climb in seven years?

_____

C. Work in pairs. Take turns telling the story of Chester Carlson's machine.

The first electronic computer was invented in 1946 at the University of Pennsylvania. Although it took the floor space of an average house, it only had the power of the pocket calculators we carry today.

Grammar Close-Up: Present Perfect Aspect (2)

For Indefinite Past Time

Use the present perfect when the time that an action took place is not known or is not important. Use the present perfect for actions that were repeated at an indefinite time in the past. Use it in contrast to the simple past for actions that were completed in past time.

EXAMPLES:

He has taken courses in English and math.
I have seen that movie three times.
Present perfect: The time (when) is not important.

He took courses in English and math. (last session)
I saw that movie three times. (before I took it back to the video store)
Simple Past: The time is mentioned or is known from the context.

Use the present form (**has**, **have**) of the auxiliary verb. Use the past participle of the main verb.

Many verbs use the past tense (regular and irregular) form of the verb as the past participle.

EXAMPLES: I have walked. I have made a mistake.
(past tense = past participle)

Other verbs use an irregular form for the past participle. Some common irregular forms of the past participle are listed below. For a complete list see Appendix 3, page 175.

Base form	Past tense	Past participle
become	became	become
begin	began	begun
blow	blew	blown
come	came	come
drink	drank	drunk
eat	ate	eaten
drive	drove	driven
give	gave	given
go	went	gone
grow	grew	grown
know	knew	known
run	ran	run
see	saw	seen
sing	sang	sung
speak	spoke	spoken
take	took	taken
wear	wore	worn
write	wrote	written

A. Choose the correct verb and put it in the present perfect form.

give   speak   wear   see   leave   write   take   drive   sing   go

1. John _____ that movie several times.
2. My brother _____ for China and Japan.
3. Janet _____ long letters to all her friends.
4. Michelle _____ some great pictures of New York.
5. I _____ to her several times.
6. Tanya _____ both trucks and jeeps.
7. Nicole _____ that jacket many times.
8. Maria and I _____ some great songs together.
9. My parents _____ on vacation for three weeks.
10. Julie _____ her sister a lot of help.

B. Choose the simple past or the present perfect form of the verb.

1. Steve (took / has taken) some good pictures with his new camera.
2. Jean and Lucie (visited / have visited) Australia last year.
3. Marc (wore / has worn) his new jacket to the party.
4. Tina (learned / has learned) to drive in high school.
5. My uncle (drank / has drunk) three cups of tea already.
6. We (spoke / have spoken) Spanish at the party last night.
7. I (wrote / have written) two letters home without an answer.
8. Annie (ate / has eaten) at my house many times.
9. Pierre (began / has begun) to speak English well.
10. Danielle (knew / has known) my sister when she lived in Quebec.

C. Complete the sentences using the simple past or the present perfect.

1. Jennifer _____ (learn) three languages.
2. Paul _____ (drive) to work last week.
3. My family _____ (visited) Greece in 1994.
4. Martin _____ (eat) Mexican food several times.
5. Jeannot _____ (worked) in a store last summer.
6. Peter _____ (go) to Malaysia several times.
7. Elaine _____ (be) to a hockey game last night.
8. Melanie and I _____ (make) dinner yesterday.
9. Patrick and Chantal _____ (fall) in love.
10. I _____ (speak) to him about it twice already.

Present Perfect for Indefinite Past Time Negative

The negative of the present perfect refers to actions or events that have not happened at the time you are speaking.

> EXAMPLE: I have been to Malaysia, but I haven't been to Australia yet.

Use **never** with the present perfect to refer to an action that has not happened **at any time**.

> EXAMPLE: He has **never** given a speech in public. (not at any time)

 Do not use **never** with a negative verb. Double negatives are not used in English.

> EXAMPLE:
> ✔ I have never eaten sushi.
> ✘ I haven't never eaten sushi.

Choose the correct verb to complete the sentences. Use the negative form of the present perfect. Use contractions.

> **leave   take   see   do   go   drink   eat   speak   begin   meet**

1. Those two _____ to each other for years.
2. We _____ anything to deserve such bad service.
3. The photographer _____ any pictures tonight.
4. Leila _____ the tea she ordered with her dinner.
5. Alex _____ any of his vegetables for some reason.
6. They _____ to talk about the real problems yet.
7. My parents _____ a movie for ages.
8. Patricia and Francine _____ each other before.
9. William _____ to the new theatre yet.
10. They are going to be late because they _____ the house yet.

Present Perfect For Indefinite Past Time Questions

Use the present perfect for questions when you don't want to focus on when an action occurred. Use the simple past when the time an action occurred is mentioned.

> EXAMPLES:
> Have you ever been to Cairo? (**at any time in your life**)
> Did you see the pyramids **when you were in Egypt**?

Ever (at any time) is often used with questions about indefinite past time. **Ever** follows the auxiliary verb and goes before the main verb.

> EXAMPLE: Have you **ever** eaten oysters? (at any time)

Complete the chart for yourself. Check the activities you have done. Then interview other students to see if they have ever done the following activities. Write their names besides the activities they have done.

	Me	Other Students
eaten oysters		
spoken in public		
smoked a cigar		
seen an eclipse		
met a famous person		
ridden a horse		
grown your hair long		
sung in public		
written a fan letter		
made a birthday cake		
been afraid of anything		
gone on a trip alone		
driven a truck		
come to class late		
taken a Spanish course		

Can Robots Think?

A. Discuss these questions.

1. What are robots?
2. What can robots do?
3. What kinds of jobs do robots do now?
4. What kinds of jobs will robots be able to do in the future?

B. Work with a partner to make predictions. Read the questions and answer **T** (true) or **F** (false).

1. Very soon we will have robots that are similar to the robots in Star Wars.

2. Some robots in existence today can think.

3. Robots have been around for more than 40 years.

4. Some of the tasks that are simplest for people are the most difficult for robots.

5. There are robots that can make financial forecasts.

6. Robots can make decisions quickly and easily.

7. Robots are being used today in the space industry and in automobile factories.

8. The robots being used today are similar to those we see in the movies.

C. Read the article quickly to check your answers.

Thinking Robots Still Missing a Few Screws

Robots have become so common in science-fiction novels and television shows that most people take the idea of artificial humanoids for granted. The real robot builders say it's not that simple. "People may think we're coming of age now, that we're going to have (Star Wars robot) R2D2 any day now," says Larry Korba, a robot expert at the National Research Council in Ottawa. "But that's just not the case. The future may look limitless but the state of the art is very crude right now. Robots can't really do any thinking at all yet."

Korba prefers to compare progress in the science of robotics—less than 40 years old—to the process of evolution, which has taken millions of years. "We're still down in the insect state—and bumblebees are way ahead of us."

Stumbling Blocks
Duplicating even the simplest human processes turned out to be far more complicated than researchers imagined when they started building robots in the 1950s.

John Tsotsos, a Toronto computer science professor who is developing a robot to help handicapped children, says the simple things—tasks most people learn early in childhood—proved the biggest stumbling blocks. "We have programs that can diagnose patients for doctors, or make accurate financial forecasts," he says. "But they can't tell a red ball sitting on a table from a green ball."

Researchers quickly ran up against a kind of "common sense" wall: robots took hours to make the simplest decisions, pondering every possibility and sifting through every bit of data. So scientists began working on getting robots to take shortcuts, including computer programs designed to make them ignore things.

Party Talk
"We call it the cocktail party effect," Tsotsos says. "It's the same ability that allows you to ignore all the conversations going on around you at a party and pay attention to just one."

Despite the problems, Korba notes there are many working robots, from the Canadarm—the robotic arm developed for NASA's space shuttle—to welding machines used on automobile assembly lines.

The U.S. army has security robots to patrol sensitive installations, and an American firm is building a robot that will serve as a hospital orderly.

Yet the imagination of sci-fi novelists continues to exceed the grasp of scientists working in the field, much to the scientists' annoyance.

"It shocks me that people actually take this stuff seriously," says Tsotsos, shaking his head. "There is a big gap between what we see in entertainment and reality—a really big gap. We're closing that gap, but slowly, very slowly. It's hard work."

Reprinted by permission of The Canadian Press

D. Read the article carefully and answer the questions.

1. Where do most people get their ideas about robots?
2. How much thinking can robots today do?
3. What are the hardest tasks for robots to do?
4. Give examples of two things robots can do.
5. Give an example of something a robot cannot do.
6. What was the "common sense" wall that robots ran up against?
7. What kind of computer programs did scientists design for robots?
8. Give three examples of work that robots are doing today.
9. What are scientists annoyed about?

Numbers and Words

Work with a partner. Write the words for each number or symbol.

Across
4. .007
9. ¼
10. 20th
11. +
12. ⅝
13. =
14. %
15. ×

Down
1. ÷
2. 0
3. ½
5. 31st
6. $
7. −
8. 19th
9. .01

Going Abroad: Capturing the Moments

Choose the best words to complete the paragraphs.

Not __1_____ people today travel without a camera. In
    (many, lots of, much)

fact, people __2_____ often identified as tourists because they
    (is, has, are)

have cameras around __3_____ necks.
    (her, our, their)

Today, __4_____ can take a picture. Cameras are
    (no one, someone, anyone)

small and easy to operate, and many are very inexpensive. Taking

pictures was not __5_____ this easy, however. In
    (never, always, sometimes)

1840, __6_____ a picture __7_____ quite difficult
    (making, taking, putting)   (had, was, were)

and time-consuming. Modern cameras snap pictures in a fraction of

a second but early cameras worked very slowly. The first cameras

__8_____ from 40 minutes to several hours to take a photo-
(made, take, took)

graph. They took so long that people who wanted to have a picture

taken __9_____ to have body supports so that they could stay
    (have, had, has)

motionless for several __10_____ .
    (minutes, hours, days)

Then in 1888, the introduction of the Kodak box camera by George

Eastman made cameras 11 _____ to everyone. Eastman
                          (available, easy, free)
designed the 12 _____ camera specifically for mass production.
                 (best, first, last)
It was easy to operate, light, and inexpensive. Photography had

entered a new age.

Never Trust a Stranger

Listening Activity 15

Episode 6: Ticket to the Temple

A. Read the paragraph quickly. Then close your book and write
while your teacher dictates.

In northern countries such as Canada or Russia, the hours of day-
light change at different times of year. In winter the hours of day-
light are short and the nights are long. In summer it is the opposite,
and it is light out from 6:00 in the morning until 9:00 or 10:00 at
night. Near the equator, night and day are equal. In tropical countries, such as Indonesia, there are 12 hours of day and 12 hours of
night all year round.

B. Read the questions aloud with a partner. Then listen and answer the questions.

1. Where are the cousins meeting Paul Hawke?

   _____

2. Why are they leaving for Borobudur at five o'clock?

   _____

3. What problem does Paul have with his wallet?

   _____

4. What does Marc suggest?

   _____

5. Why does Paul suggest they use a credit card?

   _____

6. What does Lisa discover when she looks for her card?

   _____

7. What do they think happened to Lisa's credit card?

   _____

8. What does Paul use Marc's credit card for?

   _____

9. Why does he think it is better if he goes alone to get the tickets?

   _____

10. Where does he go to get the tickets for the temple?

    _____

11. Why do they have to run when Paul comes back with the tickets?

    _____

12. Which two people take pictures with Julie's camera?

    _____

13. How long was Borobudur buried in the jungle before it became a tourist attraction?

    _____

14. Why does Julie ask if the bus is air conditioned?

    _____

15. What does Paul warn them to look out for at the temple?

    _____

C. Work in pairs. Tell each other everything you can remember about the story.

D. Write a summary of the story on a sheet of paper.

Emergency

Safety Mistakes
Vocabulary

Frozen Stiff
Reading

Calling 911
Listening Activity 16

Grammar Close-Up
Will for Future Time

Going Abroad
Hotel Fires
Vocabulary

Never Trust a Stranger
Listening Activity 17
Episode 7: Too Many Coincidences

9

Safety Mistakes

Work with a partner. Look at the picture. How many safety mistakes can you find?

Frozen Stiff

A. Discuss these questions.

1. How cold can it get during winter in Canada?
2. What can you do to protect yourself from the cold?
3. What would happen if a person were caught outside without shelter during the winter?

B. Read the story and answer the questions orally with a partner. Do not write.

Frozen Stiff

It was late at night in December of 1992. It was very cold and the roads were icy. Tanya Cooper was driving from Toronto to her parents' farmhouse near Wawa, Ontario. She had been driving for five hours, and she was getting tired.

All of a sudden, Tanya's car slid off the road and hit a snowbank. Tanya wasn't hurt, but her car was trapped. She would need a tow-truck to get out. Tanya waited in the car for help. She kept listening for the sound of traffic, but there were no other cars on the road that night. Finally she decided to walk to the nearest farmhouse.

It was –23 degrees that night, and Tanya was wearing only a winter coat and light city boots. As she walked, she began to feel very cold. Then she began to feel tired and it became difficult to keep walking. Finally, she saw a farmhouse just ahead. Tanya went towards it, but about 20 metres from the house, she collapsed in the snow.

Six hours later, Ray Pinto left his farmhouse to begin his morning chores. He found Tanya in the snow. Mr. Pinto shouted to his wife to help him take Tanya to the hospital. The problem was that they couldn't get Tanya into the car because her arms and legs were frozen stiff. They wrapped her in warm blankets and put her into the back of their truck.

At Wawa General Hospital, doctors who examined Tanya could hear only a faint heartbeat. They had to use warm water to thaw her out. She was suffering from hypothermia. Hypothermia is a condition that slows down all the body organs. It is similar to the condition of animals when they hibernate in winter. Luckily, Tanya Cooper survived. She was treated for frostbite but, miraculously, she didn't suffer any permanent damage.

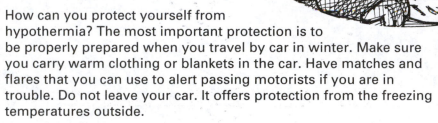

How can you protect yourself from hypothermia? The most important protection is to be properly prepared when you travel by car in winter. Make sure you carry warm clothing or blankets in the car. Have matches and flares that you can use to alert passing motorists if you are in trouble. Do not leave your car. It offers protection from the freezing temperatures outside.

C. Read the story again. Write the answers to the questions.

1. Where was Tanya Cooper travelling?
2. What happened to her car?
3. Why did she decide to walk to the nearest farmhouse?
4. What was the temperature outside?
5. What was she wearing?
6. What happened as she walked towards the farmhouse?
7. Who found Tanya, and when?
8. Why couldn't Mr. Pinto and his wife put Tanya in the car?
9. How did they take her to the hospital?
10. What was Tanya's condition when she got to the hospital?
11. What is hypothermia?
12. What was Tanya's condition afterwards?
13. What should you have in your car to protect yourself from frostbite?

The discovery of the principle of hypothermia made open-heart surgery possible. This discovery was made by a Canadian doctor, Wilfred Bigelow.

Calling 911

Listening Activity 16

A. Read the paragraph quickly. Then close your book and write while the teacher dictates.

In many towns and cities in North America, there is one number to call in emergencies. It is always the same number: 911. When you call 911, an operator will answer and ask you for some information. The operator will ask for your name and telephone number, and will inquire about the problem. Then the 911 operator will transfer your call to the police, fire department, or emergency medical services.

B. Look at the pictures and match them with the emergencies listed on page 124.

1. A burglar is breaking into a house.
2. Someone is injured and needs an ambulance.
3. A house is on fire.
4. A traffic accident has just happened.
5. A young child has wandered off.
6. Someone's cat is stuck in a tree.
7. A store is being robbed.
8. Someone is lying on the sidewalk.

C. Discuss which emergency service you would need for each emergency in the pictures. Choose the police, the fire department, or an ambulance and paramedics.

 D. Read the questions aloud with a partner. Then listen and answer the questions.

1. Where is the woman calling from?

_____

2. What is her name and how is it spelled?

_____

3. What is her address?

_____

4. Where was she when the robbery took place?

_____

5. What did she see?

_____

6. What did the first man look like? Give details.

_____

7. What did the other man look like? Give details.

_____

8. What did the robber say to the clerk?

_____

9. What happened to Mr. Lee during the robbery?

_____

10. What did the 911 operator tell the woman to do?

_____

Grammar Close-Up: "Will" for Future Time

Use **will** to predict the future, to show willingness to do something, or to make promises.

EXAMPLES:

You will be fine.

I will answer the door.

I will help you on Friday.

Use the auxiliary verb **will** before the main verb. Use the base form of the main verb. The contraction of **will** is **'ll**.

EXAMPLE: It will snow in November. It'll snow in November.

Affirmative		Contraction	
I will		I'll	
you will		you'll	
he will		he'll	
she will		she'll	
it will	stay	it'll	stay
we will		we'll	
you will		you'll	
they will		they'll	

Write these sentences in future time. Use **will**.

EXAMPLE: She plays the piano for us. She will play the piano for us.

1. It snows in Montreal in January.
2. I visit my parents at Thanksgiving.
3. She eats dinner at 8:00.
4. It is on TV at six o'clock.
5. They ate dinner in a restaurant.
6. We go to the beach in the morning.
7. I am here for the English exam.
8. He comes home at six o'clock.
9. They take a walk near the beach.
10. You watch the news on TV.

Negative

Use **not** after **will** to make a sentence negative. The contraction of **will not** is **won't**.

EXAMPLE: I will not be at home. I won't be at home.

A. Write these sentences in the negative. Use **won't**.

EXAMPLE: She will tell us her mark. **She won't tell us her mark.**

1. We will need money.
2. That bus will leave on time.
3. He will call his friend tomorrow.
4. They will tell us about it.
5. I will go out in the rain.

6. She will know about it.
7. You will be cold in that coat.
8. We will be home tonight.
9. The train will arrive on time.
10. It will rain on the weekend.

B. Look at the pictures and predict the answer.

It will rain.
It won't rain.

It will start.
It won't start.

He will miss the bus.
He won't miss the bus.

She will play tennis this afternoon.
She won't play tennis this afternoon.

She will buy a postcard.
She won't buy a postcard.

He will take a taxi.
He won't take a taxi.

C. Read and answer the questions. Use the short answer forms "Yes, (it, there, they) will" or "No, (it, there, they) won't."

The weatherman says that the temperature will go down to –18 degrees later tonight. He predicts that 25 centimetres of snow will fall by tomorrow morning. Workers will start to clear snow during the night. They probably won't finish before tomorrow afternoon. It will be hard to walk on the sidewalks. Cars won't start easily. Many people won't arrive at work on time. Late tomorrow afternoon the temperature will go up. There won't be snow on the streets and sidewalks. The city will be back to normal.

Questions

1. Will it be cold later tonight?
2. Will the temperature be below zero?
3. Will there be any snow?
4. Will workers start clearing snow in the morning?
5. Will they finish clearing snow at noon tomorrow?
6. Will it be easy to walk on the sidewalks?
7. Will cars start easily?
8. Will people be late for work?
9. Will the temperature stay down all day?
10. Will there be snow on the sidewalks at the end of the day?

Question Form

Put **will** before the subject to make a question.

EXAMPLE: Will you be there on Tuesday?

A. Make questions with the sentences. Use **will**.

1. Tom and Denis will be here soon.
2. Annie will go back to work next week.
3. You will help me find my glasses.
4. He will telephone you tomorrow.
5. She will carry it for you.
6. Robert will send us copies of the picture.
7. The car will start in cold weather.
8. Sophie and Elizabeth will choose the restaurant.
9. André will study English in Vancouver.
10. The bus will take us to the airport.

B. Match the statement and the question.

EXAMPLE: I finish at five o'clock. Will you wait for me?

1. I'll visit you at seven.
2. Her suitcase is heavy.
3. I didn't hear the weather report.
4. There will be an exam tomorrow.
5. Pablo plays the guitar very well.
6. Melanie will walk to work.
7. It's a formal party.
8. We need some dessert.
9. Janet will leave for work late tomorrow.
10. He has a good camera.

a) Will it be difficult?
b) Will you be home?
c) Will he bring his guitar to the party?
d) Will Alex make a cake?
e) Will she be on time?
f) Will he take our pictures?
g) Will it be sunny tomorrow?
h) Will she take a taxi?
i) Will the porter help her carry it?
j) Will you wear your new dress?

Going Abroad: Hotel Fires

A. Choose the best words to complete the paragraphs.

**fire   flights   room   hotel   life   passports   hotels   route
tickets   exits   smoke   inside   thousands   air   worries
elevators   travellers   key**

When most people are travelling abroad, they worry about missing
their **1**_____, forgetting their plane **2**_____or
losing their **3**_____. Something else **4**_____can
add to their list of **5**_____ is hotel fires. Every year there
are **6**_____ of fires in **7**_____.

It is important to know what to do if you are in a **8**_____
and there is a **9**_____. When you stay in a hotel, you
should learn where the **10**_____ are located. Knowing an
escape **11**_____ could save your **12**_____. If you
have to leave your room, be sure to take your **13**_____. You
may have to go back to your **14**_____ as an escape route.

Never use **15**_____ if there is a fire. You could be trapped
between floors. If there is **16**_____ in a room or corridor,
don't stand up. Smoke, like hot **17**_____, rises. It is safer to
stay near the floor and crawl out. When you are outside, never go
back **18**_____.

B. Answer the questions.

1. What are three things travellers sometimes worry about?
2. How many hotel fires are there every year?
3. Why should you know where the exits are in your hotel?
4. Why is it important to take your keys with you if there is a fire?
5. What could happen if you use an elevator during a fire?
6. Why is it safer to stay near the floor if there is a fire?
7. How should you leave the building if there is a fire?
8. What should you not do once you are outside?

Never Trust a Stranger

Listening Activity 17

Episode 7: Too Many Coincidences

A. Read the paragraph quickly. Then close your book and write while your teacher dictates.

The three cousins spent the day on a bus tour with Paul. They visited a beautiful temple and took many pictures. Now they are happy but it is very hot and they are tired. Julie has a headache and wants to rest at the hotel.

B. Work with a partner. Predict what will happen next.

C. Read the questions aloud with a partner. Then listen and answer the questions.

1. What was Julie doing in the bus?

   _____

2. What kind of show are they planning to see?

   _____

3. Why does Marc offer to take Julie to her room?

   _____

4. How will Marc find Paul and Lisa?

   _____

5. Why does Julie think that she feels sick?

   _____

6. Where does Julie think her camera is?

   _____

7. Why do they want to call Uncle Jack?

   _____

8. What does Julie think happened to her credit card?

   _____

9. Where is Marc's credit card?

   _____

10. Why does Julie suddenly have a funny feeling about Paul?

    _____

11. What happens when Marc and Julie get to the theatre?

    _____

12. What do they decide to do?

    _____

D. Close your book. Tell a partner everything you can remember about the story.

E. Write a summary of the story. Use a sheet of paper.

Getting Married

10

Weddings
Interaction
Vocabulary

Something Old, Something New...
Vocabulary
Reading

My Ideal Wedding
Discussion
Writing

Pronunciation Close-Up
Word Stress

Niagara Falls
Listening Activity 18

Grammar Close-Up
Be going to for Future Time

Going Abroad
Arranged Marriage
Vocabulary
Discussion

Never Trust a Stranger
Listening Activity 19
Episode 8: The Police Station

Weddings

A. Discuss these questions.

Think about a wedding you have been to. Describe:

- a) the ceremony
- b) the food
- c) the clothing
- d) the music
- e) the reception

B. Choose the best words to complete the paragraph.

wife   rings   finger   traditions   bride
groom   aisle   man   wedding

The wedding **1**_____ we have today originated in
many older cultures. In a modern **2**_____ ceremony,
the **3**_____ wears a white dress and walks down the
4_____ accompanied by her father. The **5**_____
wears a dark suit and is accompanied by his best **6**_____.
As the judge or religious leader pronounces them husband and
7_____, the groom puts a wedding band on the bride's
8_____, or the couple exchange **9**_____ as a
sign of enduring love. All of these customs come from the past.

C. Label the people and objects in the wedding party.

1. bride
2. groom
3. ring
4. veil
5. bridesmaid
6. best man
7. flower girl
8. bouquet
9. pageboy
10. maid of honour

Something Old, Something New...

Read the story and answer the questions that follow.

A wedding is a important event, where people dress up in special clothes and follow certain customs. Did you ever wonder where wedding traditions come from? Many of the traditions we follow today began a very long time ago. For example, many brides wear a white dress and a veil. The colour white is used as a symbol of purity and innocence. The veil began as a Greek custom designed to protect the bride from the "evil eye." What about the brides-maids who accompany the bride down the aisle? Well, this custom began in Roman times. People believed that having several young women who dressed like the bride would confuse evil spirits and chase them away from the bride.

Today a bride wears "something old, something new, something borrowed, and something blue." Something old is usually some clothing from a woman who is happily married. Something new is the wedding dress or veil the bride wears to show a new beginning. Something borrowed is often a relative's jewellery—usually gold, to represent the sun which is the source of life. Something blue represents permanence since blue is the colour of the heavens.

Not all wedding traditions have always been as refined as they are today. In the past, wedding guests did not eat the wedding cake—they threw it at the bride! The cake symbolized fertility and was an important part of the ceremony. Today, we carry on the tradition by throwing rice at the bride and groom. And in the past, the bride did not carry a bouquet of delicate flowers that she tossed to her bridesmaids at the end of the ceremony. Instead, the bride carried a bouquet made of strong herbs to scare away witches and demons. Bouquets were made of chives, rosemary, or garlic.

The tradition of the best man is very old. In the past, men in northern Europe who couldn't find a bride in their own village had to look in neighbouring villages. Since a man had no way to meet a woman, he would simply go to the next village with his friend and snatch any woman he could find walking alone. The two men had to be strong enough to carry away the woman, so a groom would choose the best man he could find to help him.

Finally, there is the custom of the wedding ring. The ring is made from the most enduring metal—gold. The circle symbolizes endless love. The tradition of wearing the ring on the fourth finger of the left hand follows ancient Greek custom. The Greeks believed that "the vein of love" ran from the fourth finger directly to the heart. Since the heart controlled both life and love, what more logical place for a promise of eternal love?

Questions

1. What did a white dress symbolize?
2. Why did Greek brides wear a veil?
3. Why did the bridesmaids dress like the bride in Roman times?
4. Match the item on the left with the meaning it represents.

   a) something old   permanence

   b) something new   happiness

   c) something borrowed life force

   d) something blue   a new start
5. Why did wedding guests throw cake at the bride?
6. Why did a bride carry garlic in her bouquet?
7. Why did men in northern Europe go to other villages to find brides?
8. What purpose did a "best man" have in the past?
9. In what two ways does a wedding ring symbolize endless love?
10. Why did the ancient Greeks put the wedding ring on the fourth finger of the left hand?

My Ideal Wedding

A. Work with a partner. Imagine that you are getting married. Discuss your ideal wedding.

a) The number of people I would like to have is…

b) The time of the day I would have the wedding is…

c) The kind of ceremony I would like is…

d) The kind of reception I would like is…

e) The kind of food I would serve is…

f) The kind of music I would like is…

g) I would wear…

h) The person I marry would wear…

i) The people I would have in my wedding party are…

j) On my honeymoon I would go to…

k) The gifts I would like to receive are…

B. Write about your ideal wedding.

When two people get married, we say they "tie the knot." The "lover's knot" has been a symbol of marriage since ancient times. It stands for love and unity. In Denmark and Holland, people actually tie two pieces of cord or ribbon together at a wedding, to symbolize the union of the bride and groom.

Pronunciation Close-Up: Word Stress

Choose the syllable that has the primary stress in the words below.

EXAMPLE: exchánges

1. tradition
2. ceremony
3. accompanied
4. originated
5. important

6. designed
7. relative
8. symbolize
9. promise
10. religious

Niagara Falls

Listening Activity 18

A. What do you know about Niagara Falls? Discuss these questions. Answer **T** (true) or **F** (false).

1. Many people go to Niagara Falls on their honeymoon.
2. Niagara Falls is located entirely in Canada.
3. Niagara Falls is the highest waterfall in the world.
4. Niagara Falls has an impressive volume of water.
5. No one has survived going over Niagara Falls in a barrel.
6. People visit Niagara Falls only in the tourist season.
7. Tourists can take a boat ride to the bottom of the falls.
8. The falls look beautiful at Christmas time.

B. Listen to the story. As you listen, check your answers to the true/false questions above.

C. Read the questions aloud with a partner. Then listen again and answer the questions.

1. What is Niagara Falls famous for?

_____

2. How many people visit Niagara Falls every year?

_____

3. Which Canadian province and American state are the falls in?

_____

4. Where does 85 percent of the water flow?

_____

5. Where is the highest waterfall in the world?

_____

6. Why is Niagara Falls impressive?

_____

7. How many cubic metres of water go over the falls every minute?

_____

8. Why did Annie Edson Taylor want to go over the falls?

_____

9. What happened to her?

_____

10. When do most people visit Niagara Falls?

_____

11. What is a popular way to see the falls?

_____

12. What does Niagara Falls look like at Christmas time?

_____

Grammar Close-Up: "Be going to" for Future Time

Use the auxiliary verb phrase **be going to** for decisions or plans for the future, for intentions for the immediate future, or for things we expect to happen immediately.

a   b   c

EXAMPLES: a) We are going to France this summer.

b) I'm going to go to bed early tonight.

c) Oops, I think that picture is going to fall.

Use the auxiliary verb phrase **be going to** before the main verb. Use the base form of the main verb.

EXAMPLE: They are going to visit Japan next summer.

Affirmative		**Contraction**	
I am going to		I'm going to	
you are going to		you're going to	
he is going to		he's going to	
she is going to	leave	she's going to	leave
it is going to		it's going to	
we are going to		we're going to	
you are going to		you're going to	
they are going to		they're going to	

A. Write sentences about the future with **be going to**.

1. Tom and Alex take pictures of the group.
2. Robert takes a taxi on Mondays.
3. They go to movies on the weekend.
4. We watch the news on TV.
5. Melanie is late for work this morning.
6. I eat lunch at the cafeteria on week days.
7. The store closes at five o'clock today.
8. Nadine and Julie play tennis near the park.
9. Fran asks the guard for information.
10. Anne goes to bed at ten o'clock.

B. Some sentences have errors. Find the errors and correct them.

1. I am going go home early today.
2. We are going to eat at seven o'clock.
3. Patricia is going play tennis this afternoon.
4. Anne is going to go to the dentist.
5. They are go to buy stamps at the post office.
6. Tom is going to send postcards to his friends.
7. Lise and Carla are going to shop downtown today.
8. Robert is going wait on the bench.
9. I am go to eat lunch in a restaurant.
10. It is going rain this afternoon.

Negative

Use **not** after the verb **be**. There are two forms of the negative contraction.

> EXAMPLES: It isn't going to rain today. It's not going to rain today.

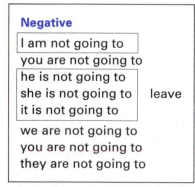

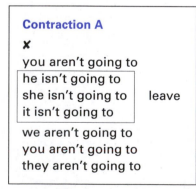

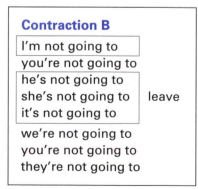

Negative		Contraction A		Contraction B	
I am not going to		✗		I'm not going to	
you are not going to		you aren't going to		you're not going to	
he is not going to		he isn't going to		he's not going to	
she is not going to	leave	she isn't going to	leave	she's not going to	leave
it is not going to		it isn't going to		it's not going to	
we are not going to		we aren't going to		we're not going to	
you are not going to		you aren't going to		you're not going to	
they are not going to		they aren't going to		they're not going to	

A. Complete the verb phrases. Use the negative form.

1. We are _____ going to watch TV this evening.
2. You are not _____ to need a coat today.
3. Annie _____ not going to get up early.
4. Lucie and Denise are not going _____ have breakfast.
5. Tom is _____ going to go to the party.
6. I _____ not going to take any money with me.
7. Carla is not _____ to wait for a bus.
8. You are not going _____ carry that box alone.
9. Nina and Alex are _____ going to come on the tour.
10. Michel is not _____ to meet us in the lobby.

B. Write the sentences in the negative. Use contractions.

1. They are going to meet us downstairs.
2. You are going to watch TV.
3. She is going to forget her purse.
4. I am going to tell him.
5. We are going to stay in this hotel.
6. They are going to play tennis today.
7. He is going to eat an orange.
8. You are going to need an umbrella.
9. I am going to stay up late.
10. She is going to cook dinner tonight.

Question Form

Put the auxiliary verb **be** before the subject to form a question with **be going to**.

EXAMPLE: Are you going to take any pictures on the trip?

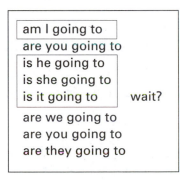

am I going to
are you going to
is he going to
is she going to
is it going to   wait?
are we going to
are you going to
are they going to

A. Make questions with these sentences.

1. Tom is going to go downtown.
2. Paul and Mario are going to meet later.
3. It is going to rain tonight.
4. We are going to enjoy that movie.

5. Robert is going to take the bus.
6. They are going to take a taxi.
7. Annie is going to buy stamps.
8. Caroline is going to drive there.
9. Daniel and Marc are going to have coffee.
10. Sylvie is going to phone you later.

B. Match the questions and the answers.

1. Where are we going to eat?
2. How are we going to get there?
3. Who is going to drive?
4. What are you going to wear?
5. What time are we going to leave?
6. Where are we going to meet?
7. Why are we going to eat in a restaurant?

a) at 7:00
b) in a restaurant
c) jeans and a shirt
d) because it's Joseph's birthday
e) on the corner
f) by car
g) Joseph is

Going Abroad:
Arranged Marriages

A. Complete the paragraphs with the words below.

**husband   parents   custom   love   families
girl   children   wealth   role**

Arranged marriage has its roots in the past when marriages were based less on **1**_____ and more on the need to build political alliances or keep **2**_____ in the family. In certain eras, young **3**_____ were betrothed to ensure solid relationships between **4**_____.

Arranged marriages also had a **5**_____ at a time when girls were married at a young age. Girls of 15 or 16 married, but didn't have life experience to choose a **6**_____. The advice of **7**_____ was a useful and important part of the process.

Today, the **8**_____ of arranging marriages survives in India, Bangladesh, Pakistan, and Sri Lanka. Many people there continue to feel that it offers better prospects for finding a suitable mate than the "boy meets **9**_____" system we have in North America.

B. Discuss the following questions.

1. What are some good criteria for choosing a mate?
2. What can you do to be sure that your marriage will last a long time?
3. What are some reasons that marriages often end in divorce?
4. Would you ask for advice before choosing a mate or would you trust your own judgment? Give reasons.

Never Trust a Stranger

Listening Activity 19

Episode 8: The Police Station

A. Work with a partner. Discuss what happened in the last episode.

B. Discuss these questions.

1. If you got lost in a strange city, what would you do?
   a) go to the police station
   b) ask a stranger for directions
   c) sit down and cry

2. If you were lost and didn't speak the language, what would you do?
   a) use sign language
   b) look at a map
   c) draw a picture

3. If you and your friend were in a strange city and your friend got lost, what would you do?
   a) call the police
   b) go and look for him or her
   c) wait at your hotel for news

4. What do you think Marc and Julie will do?
   a) call the police
   b) look for Lisa
   c) panic

C. Read the questions aloud with a partner. Then listen and answer the questions.

1. How do Marc and Julie find the police station?

   _____

2. What is Lisa doing?

   _____

3. Why isn't Lisa with Paul?

   _____

4. Why didn't she go back to the hotel?

   _____

5. What does Julie suggest that Marc do?

   _____

6. Where can they find a taxi?

   _____

7. Where was Lisa when Paul disappeared?

   _____

8. Who had Julie's camera?

   _____

9. When did Paul say he wanted to take a picture of Lisa?

   _____

10. Why is Julie sure that Paul didn't get lost?

   _____

11. What happened when Marc asked Paul questions?

    _____

12. What two things does Marc remember about Paul in the bus?

    _____

13. Where is Marc's credit card?

    _____

14. What happened to Julie's credit card?

    _____

D. Close your book. Tell your partner everything you can remember about the story.

E. Write a summary of the story.

Health and Medicine

The Incredible Human Body
Reading

The Doctor Directory
Vocabulary

The Medicine Cabinet
Reading
Vocabulary

Medical Emergencies
Listening Activity 20

Grammar Close-Up
Giving Advice Using **Should**

Grammar Close-Up
Expressing Obligation Using **Have to**

Going Abroad
Keeping Clean
Vocabulary

Never Trust a Stranger
Listening Activity 21
Episode 9: Epilogue

The Incredible Human Body

A. What do you know about the human body? Do this quiz and find out. Work with a partner. Choose the best answers.

1. Which of these elements is in the human body?
   a) carbon
   b) steel
   c) wood

2. How much of the body is water?
   a) 20 percent
   b) 50 percent
   c) 60 percent

3. How many times a day does the heart beat?
   a) 50 000
   b) 100 000
   c) 700 000

4. Blood travels through the body in the:
   a) bones
   b) ligaments
   c) blood vessels

5. Circulation of blood through the lungs takes:
   a) 1 hour
   b) 5 minutes
   c) 6 seconds

6. Which of these is called the "river of life"?
   a) blood
   b) water
   c) tears

7. How much blood is in the average body?
   a) 6 litres
   b) 12 litres
   c) 25 litres

8. How many bones are in the adult human body?
   a) 175
   b) 206
   c) 359

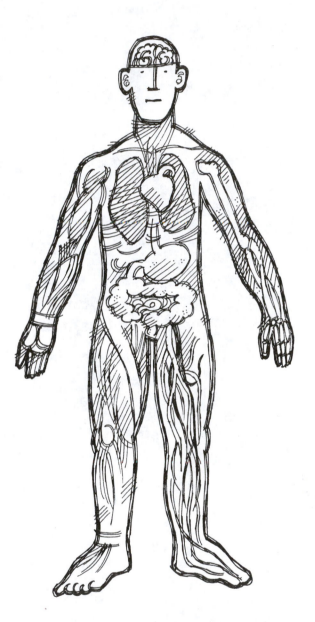

9. Who has the most bones?
   a) babies
   b) teenagers
   c) adults

10. Forty percent of the body's weight is made of:
    a) muscle
    b) skin
    c) bones

11. Which of these activities uses the most muscles?
    a) smiling
    b) frowning
    c) walking

12. How many times a day do the eye muscles move?
    a) 600
    b) 7500
    c) 100 000

13. "Taste buds" give us information about:
    a) flavour
    b) sound
    c) colour

14. Which of these is not one of the five senses:
    a) vision
    b) touch
    c) anger

15. Which sense is the least developed in human beings?
    a) smell
    b) hearing
    c) taste

16. The control and communication systems of the body are:
    a) the brain and nerves
    b) the heart and lungs
    c) the eyes and ears

17. How much does the brain weigh?
    a) 1.4 kilograms
    b) 2 kilograms
    c) 3.6 kilograms

18. The body processes food in:
    a) the skeletal system
    b) the digestive system
    c) the stomach

19. The largest organ in the human body is:
    a) the heart
    b) the lungs
    c) the skin

20. How often is the skin replaced?
    a) once a year
    b) every few months
    c) every few weeks

B. Read the text quickly. Find the answers to the quiz.

The Incredible Human Body

An athlete can run a kilometre in 4 minutes, jump over a fence that is 5 metres high, or swim across a river that is 8 kilometres wide. Feats like these are amazing, yet even simple everyday activities such as walking, writing your name, and getting dressed are coordinated by complex systems that even the most advanced robot can-not duplicate. Engineers have designed many wonderful machines, but no machine in the world comes close to the most incredible one of all: the human body.

The human body is made up of many complex systems. Your body can grow, repair itself, heal wounds, and fight infection. Every minute of the day your heart beats, sending blood containing oxygen and nourishment to each cell of the body. Your brain receives messages from your senses, and sends messages to your muscles and bones. All of these systems work together, so that you can do things such as learning a new language, designing a computer, or even flying to the moon.

You may know that the body is made of bones, muscles, blood, skin, a heart, a brain, and a nervous system. Did you know that the it also has enough fat to make up more than 8 bars of soap? Did you know that the human body has enough carbon to make the lead for 9000 pencils?

Did you know that 60 percent of the human body is water?

Every minute that we live, our hearts beat about 70 times. In a day, the heart beats about 100 000 times, and pumps about 13 640 litres of blood. The blood is pumped through about 97 000 kilometres of blood vessels. If you live to about 70 years, your heart will pump about 174 million litres of blood through your body.

The lungs are in the chest. They help us breathe by taking in oxygen and releasing carbon dioxide. In a lifetime, we will breathe over 500 million times. The lungs need blood all the time. Did you know that the circulation of blood through the lungs takes only 6 seconds?

Some people call blood "the river of life." Blood is very important to the body. It carries oxygen to every part of the body—in less than a minute! It supplies the cells of the body with water and nourishment. It takes oxygen to the lungs and removes carbon dioxide. The average body has about 6 litres of blood.

To stand, walk, or do any physical activity, we need bones and muscles. Babies have 305 bones at birth, but some of the bones fuse together as we grow. An adult has about 206 bones. The bones are moved by muscles. We have about 650 muscles, which make up 40 percent of the body's weight. To take a single step involves over 200 muscles. Did you know that frowning takes twice as many muscles as smiling? There are more than 30 muscles just in the face. It takes 34 muscles to frown, but only 15 muscles to smile.

Our five senses tell us about the world. Our ears bring us words and language, and help us distinguish over 1500 musical sounds. Our eyes let us see the world, and have colour perception so sensitive that we can differentiate as many as 300 000 different shades. Did you know that the eye muscles are the most active muscles in the body? They move an incredible 100 000 times a day or more! Three thousand taste buds tell us whether our food is sweet, sour, salty, or bitter. Even our least developed sense, smell, helps us identify thousands of different odours. Through touch, our skin gives us information about temperature and texture. It even helps us stay alive through its warning system—pain.

All of these messages speed along a network of nerves at a rate of up to 320 km/h. The information goes to the brain, which has 14 billion nerve cells ready to process information and act on it. The brain, nerves, and senses are the control and communication system of the body. The weight of an average brain is only about 1.4 kilograms, yet this small organ is the most remarkable part of the human body. The human brain controls everything from breathing and feeling to intelligence, learning, and creativity.

In order to function, the body needs fuel. We get this fuel through the foods we eat. The digestive system, which measures about 9 metres in total, is the fuel-processing plant for the body. Here, food is broken down to be used to build and repair the body, and to give us energy. During an average lifetime, a person eats as much as 50 tonnes of food and drinks as much as 45 000 litres of liquid.

All of the body systems are held together by another system. This system bends, grows, and is even waterproof. It is our skin, the largest organ in the human body. The average person has 2 square metres of skin. Each piece of skin that is about 2 centimetres square has more than 3 million cells, a metre of blood vessels, 35 nerve-endings, and 80 sweat glands. Every few weeks, the skin wears away, and is replaced by new skin.

The human body has many separate parts that work together in miraculous ways. What a wonderful machine!

The Doctor Directory

Which specialty does each doctor treat? Work with a partner.
Match the doctor to the specialty.

1. Orthopedists
2. Pediatrician
3. Radiologist
4. Allergist
5. Dermatologist
6. Cardiologist
7. Dentist
8. Gerontologist
9. Psychiatrist
10. Obstetrician
11. Hematologist
12. Ophthalmologist

a) old age
b) the eyes
c) the skin
d) the mind
e) bones and muscles
f) the teeth
g) allergies
h) pregnancy
i) children
j) X-rays
k) the heart
l) the blood

The Medicine Cabinet

Read the labels for the medications on pages 150 and 151. Then
work with a partner to answer the questions.

1. What are the symptoms of a cold or 'flu? Which medications
   are recommended for these symptoms?
2. Which medications can you take for pain?
3. If pain or fever persists, how long should you wait before consulting your physician?
4. What does "Do not exceed recommended dosage" mean?
5. Name some health conditions under which a person should not
   take cold medicine.
6. At what age does a person begin to take an adult dose of
   medicine?
7. Can children under two years of age take medication for
   motion sickness?
8. Which medications can cause sleepiness?
9. What kind of food or drink should be avoided when taking
   medications that can cause drowsiness?
10. What activities should be avoided when taking medications
    that cause drowsiness? Why?

11. Which medications contain enough drugs to harm a child seriously?

12. Which medication can cause excitability in children?

13. Which medications should not be used by women who are pregnant or nursing a baby?

14. What should you do if the end flap of the carton is open? Why?

15. Which medications should not be taken if you are already taking another medication?

16. Complete the information for Reyes syndrome.
    a) What is Reyes syndrome?
    b) Who can get it?
    c) Which medication should be avoided in connection with this disease?

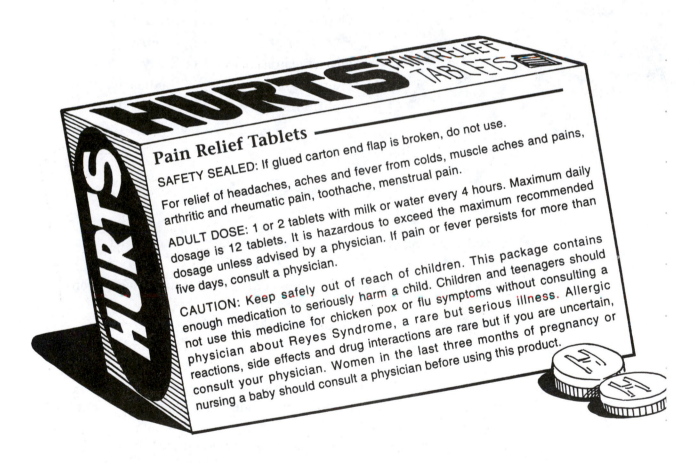

Pain Relief Tablets

SAFETY SEALED: If glued carton end flap is broken, do not use.

For relief of headaches, aches and fever from colds, muscle aches and pains, arthritic and rheumatic pain, toothache, menstrual pain.

ADULT DOSE: 1 or 2 tablets with milk or water every 4 hours. Maximum daily dosage is 12 tablets. It is hazardous to exceed the maximum recommended dosage unless advised by a physician. If pain or fever persists for more than five days, consult a physician.

CAUTION: Keep safely out of reach of children. This package contains enough medication to seriously harm a child. Children and teenagers should not use this medicine for chicken pox or flu symptoms without consulting a physician about Reyes Syndrome, a rare but serious illness. Allergic reactions, side effects and drug interactions are rare but if you are uncertain, consult your physician. Women in the last three months of pregnancy or nursing a baby should consult a physician before using this product.

GRAVEL

MOTION SICKNESS TABLETS

Motion Sickness Tablets

For prevention of nausea, dizziness and vomiting, take tablets 30 minutes before departure.

DOSAGE: **Adults:** For relief of nausea, vomiting or dizziness, 1 to 2 tablets every 4 hours as needed, up to 8 tablets in 24 hours. **Juniors 6 to 12 years:** 1/2 to 1 tablet every 6 to 8 hours as needed, up to a maximum of 3 tablets in 24 hours. **Children 2 to 6 years:** 1/4 to 1/2 tablet every 6 to 8 hours as needed, up to 1 1/2 tablets in 24 hours. **Infants 0 to 2 years:** as directed by physician.

CAUTION: Do not exceed recommended dosage. THIS PRODUCT MAY CAUSE DROWSINESS. DO NOT DRIVE A MOTOR VEHICLE OR PERFORM TASKS REQUIRING MENTAL ALERTNESS OR CONCENTRATION. Prolonged use on physician's advice only.

Avoid alcoholic beverages. Do not take if you have: glaucoma, chronic lung disease, difficulty in urination due to an enlargement of the prostate gland, or if you are pregnant or breast-feeding unless directed by a physician. Do not take with other antihistamines, tranquilizers or any other sedatives without consulting your physician. Note: This medication may cause excitability, especially in children.

KEEP OUT OF THE REACH OF CHILDREN.

ACH-OO-OO-OO

COLD MEDICINE TABLETS
COLD MEDICINE

Cold Medicine

FOR RELIEF OF COLD/FLU SYMPTOMS

Relieves sniffles and sneezing, calms and quiets coughing, eases head and body aches, relieves nasal and sinus congestion, reduces fever, relieves minor sore throat pain.

DOSAGE: Adults (ages 12 and over) take one capsule every 12 hours.

CAUTION: Do not exceed recommended dosage. Do not take this product for more than 7 days. Consult a physician if symptoms do not improve or are accompanied by high fever, or if cough worsens. Children under 12, elderly persons, pregnant or nursing women, persons with high blood pressure, thyroid problems, chronic lung disease or shortness of breath, heart disease, diabetes, glaucoma, depression, prostate gland enlargement, asthma, or persons under treatment for depression or using anti-depressant medications should use only under the direction of a physician.

May cause marked drowsiness. Alcohol may increase the drowsiness effect. Avoid alcoholic beverages. Do not drive or engage in activities requiring alertness until response is determined. As with any drug, if pregnant or nursing a baby, consult a health professional before using this product.

KEEP THIS AND ALL DRUGS OUT OF REACH OF CHILDREN. THIS PACKAGE CONTAINS ENOUGH MEDICINE TO SERIOUSLY HARM A CHILD.

Medical Emergencies

Listening Activity 20

A. Work with a partner. Find these items in the picture:

**stretcher   wheelchair   walker   sling   crutches
cane   cast   bandage**

 B. Read the questions aloud with a partner. Then listen and answer the questions.

1. What are two main reasons people go to the emergency room of a hospital?
2. What kind of injuries do people often have?

3. What are some illnesses that bring people to the emergency room?

4. What kind of leg or foot injury should be seen at the hospital?

5. When you arrive in Emergency, who will see you first?

6. What does a triage nurse do?

7. Who will be seen first by the doctor?

8. What should you do if you need follow-up after an emergency-room visit?

9. What happens if you don't have a family physician?

10. Where can you get medications prescribed by the emergency-room physician?

Grammar Close-Up: Giving Advice Using "Should"

Use **should** to give advice or express opinions. Use the negative form, **should not**, to advise against doing something. The contraction of **should not** is **shouldn't**.

> EXAMPLES: You should see a doctor. (It is my opinion.)
>
> People shouldn't smoke. (Doctors advise against it.)

Affirmative	Negative	Contraction
I should	I should not	I shouldn't
you should	you should not	you shouldn't
he should	he should not	he shouldn't
she should go	she should not go	she shouldn't go
it should	it should not	it shouldn't
we should	we should not	we shouldn't
you should	you should not	you shouldn't
they should	they should not	they shouldn't

A. Match the problem with the solution.

1. a headache
2. feeling tired
3. want to lose weight
4. a broken arm
5. a cut finger
6. the 'flu
7. trouble reading
8. a sprained ankle
9. afraid of sunburn
10. feeling thirsty

a) get an X-ray
b) eat less
c) see an eye doctor
d) use crutches
e) take an aspirin
f) have a drink of water
g) sleep in tomorrow
h) get stitches
i) use sunscreen
j) take aspirin, drink juice, stay in bed

B. Write sentences giving advice for these problems. Use **should** or **shouldn't**.

1. Suddenly I'm feeling extremely hungry.
2. The weather report says it will be very cold outside tomorrow.
3. Doctors say that smoking is very dangerous to our health.
4. I don't really like hot days very much. I prefer cold weather.
5. I slipped on the ice and hurt my ankle.
6. Someone told me that that movie is really boring.
7. I'm exhausted from cross-country skiing all afternoon.
8. Reading in poor light can harm your eyes.
9. I really like to ski in the Rockies more than in the Adirondacks.
10. I have a sore throat and a cough.

Grammar Close-Up: Expressing Obligation Using "Have to"

Use **have to** to express obligations or things that it is necessary for you to do.

EXAMPLES: Mike has to be at work at nine o'clock. (It's a company rule.)
I have to go now. (I'm tired.)

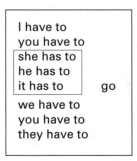

I have to
you have to
she has to
he has to
it has to   go
we have to
you have to
they have to

A. Andrew is leaving on a trip to Indonesia. Gaby is asking him questions about his arrangements. Match the questions with the answers.

1. What do you have to do before you leave?
2. Why do you have to get a visa to go to Indonesia?
3. What time do you have to be at the airport?
4. Why do you have to be there so early if the plane leaves at 10:00?
5. What time do you have to wake up to be at the airport on time?
6. What do you have to do when you get to the airport?
7. Where do you have to go to check in for your flight?
8. What do you have to do to get your boarding pass?
9. Who do you have to show your boarding pass to?
10. Do you have to change planes during the trip?

a) I have to be there at 7 o'clock.
b) Yes, I have to change planes in Chicago and Tokyo.
c) I have to check in with the airline.
d) I have to get a visa.
e) I have to wake up at 5.30 a.m.
f) ...because the Indonesian government requires it.
g) I have to show it to the security guard.
h) I have to go to the airline counter.
i) I have to show them my airline ticket.
j) ...because it is an international flight.

B. Complete the sentences with the correct form of **have to**.

1. Passengers _____ pass through security checks at the airport.
2. All the window seats are taken. That man _____ take an aisle seat.
3. Everyone _____ fasten his or her seat belt during take off.
4. You _____ check in at Gate 97 half an hour before your flight.
5. You _____ stow all hand baggage under the seats before takeoff.
6. Passengers _____ check their baggage before boarding the plane.
7. Mrs. James _____ pay to leave her car in the airport parking garage.
8. International passengers _____ have their customs forms stamped.
9. Passengers _____ wait at the carrousel for their baggage.
10. Rick is a vegetarian. He _____ order his meals in advance.

Going Abroad: Keeping Clean

Use these words to complete the paragraphs.

**beliefs   faces   clean   bathing   wounds   dangerous
soap   health   wash   year   medicine**

The ancient Greeks knew that it was important to keep the body
__1_____, and soap was especially useful for cleaning
__2_____. So in Greece, soap was used not only for
personal cleanliness, but was actually considered a __3_____.

People did not always have these __4_____, however. Did you know that at certain times in history, people thought that __5_____ the body was dangerous to the __6_____? During the Middle Ages in Europe, people did not __7_____ very often. In fact, they feared __8_____ and water. People thought that it was __9_____ to wash too often—that is, more than once a month, or even once a __10_____. Most people did not even wash their __11_____ for weeks on end!

Never Trust a Stranger

Listening Activity 21

Episode 9: Epilogue

A. What do you remember? Think about the story and try to answer the questions **T** (true) or **F** (false) with a partner.

1. Lisa lost her credit card at the hotel in Hong Kong.
2. Paul Hawke is a businessman from Singapore.
3. Paul Hawke could speak Indonesian.
4. Paul Hawke invited Marc, Julie, and Lisa to see the temple at Borobudur.
5. Marc lent his credit card to Paul Hawke.
6. Julie had her camera stolen during the visit to Borobudur.
7. Julie's credit card was stolen by a pickpocket.
8. Lisa was in the police station because she was arrested.
9. Paul Hawke is in the import-export business.
10. Julie has a funny feeling about Paul Hawke.

B. Read the questions aloud with a partner. Then listen and answer the questions.

1. What did the cousins do about their credit cards?

   _____

2. When did Marc hear the radio broadcast?

   _____

3. Who was arrested at Tang's Department Store?

   _____

4. Who were the men who were arrested?

   _____

5. Where were the tourists who were robbed travelling to?

   _____

6. Which cities had reports about the gang filed with the police?

   _____

7. How did the gang take credit cards without being noticed?

   _____

8. What story would the good-looking young man tell people, in order to get their credit cards?

   _____

9. What aliases did the gang leader use?

   _____

10. What would the gang do with the stolen credit cards?

   _____

11. Who was the young woman Hall offered to take to the Juorng Bird Sanctuary?

   _____

12. What do police in Hong Kong and Vancouver want to talk to the gang leader about?

   _____

13. What warning is given to travellers in international airports?

   _____

C. Discuss the story with a partner.

D. Write a summary of the story's ending.

The Great Outdoors

Camping
Discussion

Survival in the Wilds
Interaction
Reading

Moose on the Loose
Listening Activity 22

Going Abroad
Migration
Vocabulary

Grammar Close-Up
Conditional Sentences (Type I)

12

Camping

Discuss these questions.

1. Have you ever been camping? Where did you go?
2. What kind of equipment do you need to camp out?
3. What kind of supplies should you bring?
4. What kind of problems can people have when they go camping?
5. What kind of safety precautions should you take when you go camping?
6. What should you do if someone gets hurt when you go camping?

Survival in the Wilds

Imagine that you and a friend are lost in the wilds. You don't know how long it will take for rescuers to find you. Would you survive?

Work in a group to do this quiz. Then read the information on page 170 to find out your chances for survival.

1. You are lost in the wilds. What is your greatest danger?
   a) lack of food and water
   b) wild animals
   c) panic

2. You think your friend may be in shock. The symptoms of shock are:
   a) high fever
   b) sweating, trembling
   c) agitation

3. The treatment for shock is:
   a) vigorous exercise
   b) rest near a campfire
   c) to elevate your head

4. You are caught in a thunderstorm. You should take shelter:
   a) in an open field
   b) under a small evergreen tree
   c) under a large maple tree

5. You have to cross a lake that is covered with ice. The areas to avoid are:
   a) dark patches
   b) light patches
   c) uneven areas

6. Which body parts are most vulnerable to frostbite?
   a) the ears
   b) the nose
   c) the legs

7. The best treatment for frostbite is to:
   a) rub the spot with snow
   b) use body heat to warm the area
   c) make faces or slap the skin

8. Which of these are effective ways to avoid mosquito bites?
   a) use an electronic mosquito repeller
   b) apply a bug repellent cream
   c) tuck in your shirt and pants

9. Which animals pose the greatest danger to people?
   a) grizzly bears
   b) raccoons
   c) wolves

10. You see a bear approaching. You should:
    a) stop moving
    b) run as fast as you can
    c) attack it with a stick

11. You have only a little food. You should eat:
    a) mostly protein
    b) mostly carbohydrates
    c) mostly dried food

12. You have very little food. Which plants are safe to eat?
    a) dandelions
    b) mushrooms
    c) clover

13. You are desperate for food. Which animals are easy to catch?
    a) insects
    b) frogs
    c) a moose

14. You are lost in an area with few trees. It is very hot. You should:
    a) stay put and wait for rescue
    b) try to collect water
    c) sleep during the day and look for help at night

15. You develop blisters on your feet from walking. You should:
    a) apply band aids or soft material
    b) apply heat
    c) try to burst them

16. The most common poisonous plants have:
    a) small white or light-coloured berries
    b) large green leaves
    c) red flowers

17. You touch poison ivy or another poisonous plant. You should:
    a) wash right away
    b) drink lots of water
    c) change your clothes

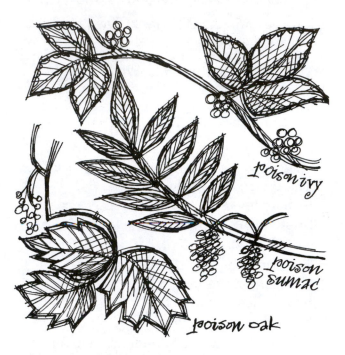

18. You need to build a fire. You have no matches. You can:
    a) use a camera lens
    b) use glasses
    c) rub two sticks together

19. You come to a stream. You probably should not drink the water if:
    a) it is moving quickly
    b) there are no plants growing near it
    c) it has a strong mineral taste

20. You are driving your car on a lonely country road when there is a severe snowstorm. You should:
    a) shout for help
    b) try to walk to the nearest town
    c) stay in your car

Turn to page 170 to check your answers.

oose on the Loose

Listening Activity 22

A. Discuss these questions.

1. What are some big animals that live in the woods?
2. What does this road sign mean?
3. What would happen if a car hit a moose?

B. Listen to the information. After you listen, work in pairs. Put the main ideas in the chart.

	Moose story 1	**Moose story 2**
Province		
Location of moose		
Number of moose		
Solution		

C. Read the questions aloud with a partner. Then listen again and answer the questions.

1. Why do we see road signs warning us of a moose crossing?
   _____

2. Where do moose live?
   _____

3. How much can a moose weigh?
   _____

4. How tall can a moose be?
   _____

5. How can you tell a male moose from a female moose?
   _____

6. Why do we sometimes see moose where we least expect them?
   _____

7. What were people in New Brunswick worried about?
   _____

8. Why did the moose in New Brunswick come onto the highway at night?

   _____

9. What idea did people have?

   _____

10. What woke the family in Ottawa up?

    _____

11. How did the moose get into the swimming pool?

    _____

12. Who did the family call for help?

    _____

13. How did the moose get on TV?

    _____

14. Explain how the moose got back to the forest.

    _____

D. Tell the moose stories to your partner. Then your partner will tell you the stories.

E. Write everything you can remember about the moose stories.

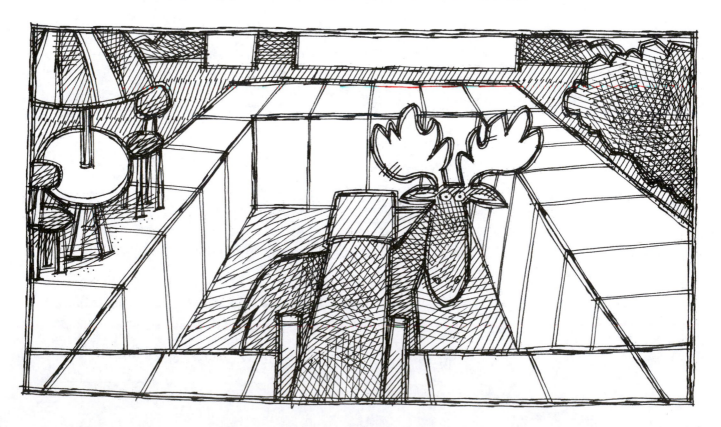

Going Abroad: Migration

A. Work with a partner. Read the statements about migration. Write **T** (true) or **F** (false).

1. Birds and animals migrate because of the climate.
2. Most animals that migrate are small, like birds.
3. Most animals that migrate go south in the winter.
4. Birds usually migrate in the summer and winter.
5. Animals stay together in families when they migrate.
6. Fish can migrate between fresh water and salt water.
7. Whales have protection from the cold so they don't migrate.

B. Complete the paragraphs with the words below.

> groups   caribou   summer   fall   birds   herds   days
> salmon   spring   bird   water   south   winter   salt
> animals   food   boats   fresh

Many animals in Canada migrate. Some __1_____ migrate because of the climate. They live in Canada in the __2_____ and summer and fly __3_____ to warmer climates in the __4_____ and winter. One kind of __5_____ flies from the Arctic Ocean to the Antarctic Ocean when it migrates. That's a record.

Other 6_____, such as the caribou, migrate to find
7_____. They migrate when they have eaten all the food
in one location. Caribou migrate in large 8_____ called
herds. Some 9_____ have up to a million 10_____
in them. When all these caribou cross a river, they can take a very
long time. During a caribou migration, 11_____ on some
northern rivers have to stop for 12_____ while the caribou
cross night and day.

Whales spend 13_____ in the Arctic Ocean and then
move down the Pacific coast in 14_____. They spend
winter in the warm 15_____ off the coast of California.
16_____ migrate from the 17_____ water streams
where they are born and have babies in the 18_____ water in
warmer climates.

C. Read the text and check your answers for Exercise A.

Grammar Close-Up: Conditional Sentences (Type I)

Use a conditional sentence to show an **if/then** relationship between
two actions. Use Type I conditional for real future possibility. The **if**
clause gives the condition that will make a future action possible.

> EXAMPLE: If X happens, then Y will happen.

The **if** clause can be first or last in the sentence with no change in
meaning.

> EXAMPLES: If it rains, we will go.
>   We will go if it rains.

A. Match the clauses to make logical sentences.

1. If it snows tonight,	a) you will play well.
2. If the bus is late,	b) you can have a snack.
3. If we study hard,	c) we will feel rested.
4. If we have enough players,	d) they will phone.
5. If you are hungry,	e) we will have good marks.
6. If we sleep late,	f) I will take it.
7. If the phone rings,	g) I will answer it.
8. If they are late,	h) we will have a team.
9. If the ticket is still available,	i) we will take a taxi.
10. If you practice enough,	j) the streets will be dangerous.

B. Match the clauses to make logical sentences.

1. He will be hungry
2. They will come for sure
3. We will be tired
4. It will snow later today
5. She will probably work harder
6. Our rent will go up
7. The schools will close tomorrow
8. We will arrive on time
9. Our holidays will be a lot of fun
10. I will be bored on Saturday

a) if we stay up until midnight.
b) if she gets an increase in salary.
c) if there is a snow storm.
d) if you invite them to the party.
e) if we go to Mexico.
f) if I stay home all day.
g) if we take a taxi.
h) if the landlord does repairs.
i) if he misses his lunch break.
j) if the temperature continues to go down.

The **if** clause describes a condition that is necessary for something to happen. Use present time for the **if** clause. The main clause describes what will happen in future. Use future time for the main clause.

EXAMPLE: If it **rains**, we **will take** an umbrella.

present   future

C. Put the verbs in the correct tense.

1. If the moose _____ (jump) over that fence, it _____ (fall) in the pool.

2. Someone _____ (buy) the food if we _____ (make) a list.

3. Janet _____ (arrive) late if there _____ (be) a snow storm.

4. If someone _____ (be) hurt, another person _____ (call) a doctor.

5. If we _____ (see) a bear in the woods we _____ (lie down) and not move.

6. If we _____ (have) no food left, we _____ (eat) some plants.

7. If you _____ (touch) poison ivy, you _____ (get) a rash.

8. If it _____ (start) to rain very hard, the campers _____ (stay) in their tents.

9. We _____ (get lost) if Jack _____ (forget) to bring the maps.

10. If someone _____ (hit) a moose, they _____ (damage) their car badly.

Negative

One or both clauses in a conditional sentence can be negative. The **if** clause is in present time and the main clause is in future time. The negative form of **will** is **won't** (**will not**).

EXAMPLES:
    If it rains, we won't go.
    If it doesn't rain, we will go.
    If it isn't sunny, we won't go.

A. Put the verb in the main clause in the negative form.

1. If it rains, we will go to the picnic.
2. If the pay is low, I will accept that job.
3. The team will win, if their best player is injured.
4. My brother will change jobs if he gets a raise in pay.
5. I will be late for work if I leave immediately.
6. If they rent two movies, they will go to bed early.
7. If he is really tired, he will stay up late.
8. If her knapsack is heavy, she will carry it herself.
9. The elevator will work well if it is overloaded.
10. The car will start easily if it is –32 degrees.

B. Choose correct endings for these sentences.

1. If you get to the campsite late,
    a) you'll find a spot.
    b) you won't find a spot.

2. If you buy your supplies before you leave,
    a) you won't run out of food.
    b) you'll run out of food.

3. If you aren't careful,
    a) you won't get hurt.
    b) you'll get hurt.

4. If he smokes cigarettes,
    a) he'll stay healthy.
    b) he won't stay healthy.

5. If they don't practise,
    a) they will win the game.
    b) they won't win the game.

6. If they don't hurry up,
    a) they won't be on time.
    b) they'll be on time.

7. If he doesn't stop smoking,
    a) it will affect his health.
    b) it won't affect his health.

8. If I don't wash the dishes,
    a) my mother will be happy.
    b) my mother won't be happy.

9. If the temperature goes down,
    a) we'll need coats.
    b) we won't need coats.

10. If they drive carelessly,
    a) they'll have an accident.
    b) they won't have an accident.

C. Put the verbs in the correct tense.

1. If you don't go, everyone _____ (be) sad.
2. The party will be a success if everyone _____ (come).
3. Rick won't serve meat, if you _____ (be) vegetarian.
4. If you work hard, you _____ (pass) the exam.
5. If Susan hears the bell, she _____ (answer) the door.
6. If Nicole and Shirley are late again , I _____ (say) something.
7. We won't have the exam, if anybody _____ (be) absent.
8. Gaby will let us know if she _____ (gets) an answer.
9. If the phone rings, someone _____ (hear) it.
10. If she doesn't understand me, I _____ (speak) more slowly.

Question Form

The main clause can be a question about the future. The **if** clause is always in present time.

> EXAMPLES: Will they cancel the picnic if it rains?
>
> If we are late, will they let us in?

A. Match the two parts of the sentence.

1. What will we wear	a) if we don't study?
2. Will the teacher be angry	b) will people understand us?
3. If it snows tomorrow,	c) if we go to the party?
4. If we speak English,	d) if the airline loses their luggage?
5. How will we pass the exam	e) if we forget our homework?
6. Will they go to the beach	f) will the schools be closed?
7. If it doesn't rain,	g) if it's cold tomorrow?
8. If I exercise every day,	h) what will happen to the garden?
9. If the phone rings,	i) will you hear it?
10. What will they do	j) will I have more energy?

B. Choose the correct question word.

1. If we don't do our homework, (what/how) will anyone know?
2. (Who/How) will know if we are late for class?
3. (What/Where) will you do if you run out of money?
4. If the teacher is absent, (what/who) will teach the class?
5. If we don't have bus tickets, (where/how) will we get home?
6. (When/what) will we study, if we go to a movie tonight?
7. (Where/how) will we get to class, if it snows tomorrow?
8. If it rains, (what/where) will we have the picnic?
9. (What/who) will help us if we don't understand the homework?
10. If it's cold tomorrow, (what/how) will we wear?

Survival in the Wilds

Read the information to check your answers to the quiz on page 161.

1. Panic is your greatest danger. Of course, telling someone not to panic is easy advice to give, but difficult advice to follow. The problem, however, is that when you panic, you are likely to act wildly, and get yourself into a worse situation than before.

2. Shock is a physical reaction to an injury. Sweating, trembling, and pale skin are symptoms. A person in shock may also be thirsty and have a rapid pulse.

3. The treatment for shock is rest and warmth. The victim should lie down with feet elevated, beside a fire if possible, and away from the wind. Try to help the victim relax as much as possible.

4. If you are caught in a thunderstorm, take shelter under a small tree, rather than a large one, to minimize the danger from lightning.

5. Frozen lakes can have patches of thin ice. Avoid dark patches on light-coloured ice, as these are danger areas. Spring is the most unpredictable time of year, so avoid travelling on ice if possible at this time.

6. The face, hands, and feet are farthest away from the heart. In cold temperatures, circulation to the extremities is cut down, and these body parts are not kept properly warm. When the skin begins to freeze, greyish or yellow-white areas may form on the fingers, nose, etc. You can see the spots before you feel anything. This frozen skin is called frostbite.

7. To treat frostbite, do not rub it with snow, as this will actually make it worse. Skin that has frostbite is injured and must be treated gently. Warm the skin in any way you can: put warm clothes on it, cup your hands over a frozen ear, etc. Even making faces, slapping your skin, or chewing gum helps maintain circulation to the affected areas.

8. Electronic mosquito repellers are not very effective, and the batteries wear out very quickly. Bug repellent cream is better. Also, be sure to cover up with long sleeves. Tuck your shirt into your pants, and tuck your pants into your socks, to avoid exposing skin to the mosquitoes.

9. Contrary to popular opinion, wolves are not generally dangerous to people. In fact, most North American animals do not pose a danger. The exceptions are grizzly and polar bears. However, in areas where animals encounter humans, such as in parks, the animals may no longer be afraid of people, and may act unpredictably.

10. If you encounter a bear, stop moving. If you move suddenly, or try to run away, the bear may perceive your movement as an attack, and will fight back. If you remain motionless, the animal will eventually lose interest and leave.

11. If you have food with you, eat sparingly. Try to eat mostly carbohydrates (for example, bread). Protein and dried or dehydrated foods actually take water from the body in the process of digestion.

12. Clover and dandelions are plants that you can find in many places. It may seem that these plants are better suited to cows, but when you are very hungry, they may save your life. The plants are completely edible, including the roots and flowers. You can eat clover raw, but dandelions are best boiled, as they have a bitter taste. Never eat mushrooms. Even experts have difficulty telling which ones are poisonous, and mushrooms have almost no food value anyway.

13. Large animals such as moose are very difficult to catch. Eating insects may not seem very enticing, but if you are faced with severe hunger pains, you will not be too fussy about where your food comes from. Most insects are easy to catch and edible, and are actually food delicacies in different parts of the world. Frogs are also easy to catch, especially at night. In France, people consider frogs' legs a delicious treat.

14. If you are in an extremely hot place, do not stay put and wait for rescue, unless you know that the area is well patrolled. You should avoid walking in the daytime, however. Rest during the day, preferably under some shade, and walk at night when the air is cooler.

15. If you have to walk long distances, blisters may develop very quickly and can be quite painful. Check your feet regularly for red, irritated patches. Apply band aids or any soft material such as leaves or moss to cushion your skin. If you have blisters, do not burst them, as this makes the pain worse and increases the chance of infection.

16. Three kinds of poisonous plants are quite common and can give you a lot of trouble. They are poison ivy, poison oak, and poison sumac. They all have small white or light greyish green berries. If you come in contact with these plants, you can experience itching, redness, and blistering.

17. If you touch one of these plants, you should wash right away with soap and water, if possible. Be particularly careful not to touch your eyes, as the juice from the berries can be dangerous to the eyes.

18. If you have no matches, you need to find another way to start a fire. You will probably not be able to create fire by rubbing two sticks together, unless you have practice at doing this. Eye glasses can be used, but only glasses worn by a farsighted person will work. Glasses from a nearsighted person don't work because the lenses will not focus light to a point. A camera lens can be used in bright sunlight, by focusing the sunlight through the lens, which is pointed at dry wood.

19. Water that is fast moving, especially from mountain streams, can be trusted more than slow-moving rivers. Green plants growing near the water also indicate that the water is safe. If there are no plants growing nearby, this is an indication that toxic chemicals may be in the water. Don't worry if the water tastes of minerals, or is not crystal clear, however. This does not mean that the water is unfit to drink.

20. The car is an ideal shelter. You can run the motor for ten minutes every hour to keep warm, and get water to drink by melting snow with the heat of the engine. Don't try to reach help by walking. Without proper clothing and nourishment, it is easy to be overcome with exhaustion from walking through deep snow.

Appendix 1: Spelling Verb Forms Ending "ing"

The spelling rules for continuous verbs are different from the rules for regular past tense verbs. For example, with the verb **try**, the past tense is **tried**, but the continuous tense is **trying**.

Rule 1 Verbs that end with **e** drop the **e** and add **ing**:

write   writing

Rule 2 Verbs that end with two consonants (**n,d,k, b**, etc.) or with two vowels (**a,e,i,o,u**) add **ing**:

try   trying
read   reading

Rule 3 Verbs that end with a vowel and a consonant double the final letter and add **ing**:

put   putting

Exceptions: consonants **w**, **x**, and **y**. (**buy   buying**)

Appendix 2: Spelling Simple Past Tense

2 consonants	add **ed**	work	work**ed**
2 vowels + consonant	add **ed**	need	need**ed**
vowel + **y**	add **ed**	play	play**ed**
consonant + **y**	change **y** to **i** add **ed**	try	tri**ed**
vowel + consonant	double consonant add **ed**	plan	plan**ned**

Not all verbs that end in vowel + consonant double the final letter. Common exceptions are **listened**, **opened**, **answered**.

Appendix 3: Irregular Past Tense and Past Participle Forms

Many past participles are the same as the regular or irregular past tense forms. Irregular past participles are shown in bold type below.

Present	Past	Past participle
arise	arose	**arisen**
awake	awoke	**awaken**
be	was, were	**been**
beat	beat	**beaten**
become	became	**become**
begin	began	**begun**
bite	bit	**bitten**
bleed	bled	bled
blow	blew	**blown**
break	broke	**broken**
bring	brought	brought
build	built	built
buy	bought	bought
catch	caught	caught
choose	chose	**chosen**
come	came	**come**
cost	cost	cost
cut	cut	cut
dig	dug	dug
do	did	**done**
draw	drew	**drawn**
drink	drank	**drunk**
drive	drove	**driven**
eat	ate	**eaten**
fall	fell	**fallen**
feed	fed	fed
feel	felt	felt
find	found	found
fly	flew	**flown**
forbid	forbade	**forbidden**
forget	forgot	**forgotten**
forgive	forgave	**forgiven**
freeze	froze	**frozen**
get	got	**gotten** (got)
give	gave	**given**
go	went	**gone**
grow	grew	**grown**
have	had	had
hear	heard	heard
hide	hid	**hidden**

Present	Past	Past participle
hit	hit	hit
hold	held	held
hurt	hurt	hurt
keep	kept	kept
know	knew	**known**
lay	laid	laid
lead	led	led
leave	left	left
let	let	let
lie	lay	**lain**
lose	lost	lost
make	made	made
mean	meant	meant
meet	met	met
pay	paid	paid
put	put	put
read	read	read
ride	rode	**ridden**
ring	rang	**rung**
rise	rose	**risen**
run	ran	run
see	saw	**seen**
sell	sold	sold
send	sent	sent
shake	shook	**shaken**
shine	shone	shone
shoot	shot	shot
show	showed	shown
shrink	shrank	**shrunk**
shut	shut	shut
sing	sang	**sung**
sit	sat	sat
sleep	slept	slept
speak	spoke	**spoken**
spread	spread	spread
spring	sprang	**sprung**
stand	stood	stood
steal	stole	**stolen**
stink	stank	**stunk**
swear	swore	**sworn**
swim	swam	**swum**
take	took	taken
teach	taught	taught
tear	tore	**torn**
tell	told	told
think	thought	thought
throw	threw	**thrown**
understand	understood	understood
wake	woke	**woken**
wear	wore	**worn**
win	won	won
write	wrote	**written**